don't call me PREACHER

for Laymen and Other Ministers

by Phil Barnhart

WILLIAM B. EERDMANS PUBLISHING COMPANY
Grand Rapids, Michigan

An Eerdmans special edition published by arrangement with Forum House Publishers, Atlanta, containing the complete text of the original hard-cover edition

Copyright © 1972 by Forum House
Forum House edition published December 1972

Eerdmans edition published December 1972

Printed in the United States of America

Library of Congress catalog card number: 72-87066
ISBN: 0-8028-1517-0

Contents

Introduction

People who have heard about this book have asked what it is about and I've wondered what to say. The most truthful answer is, "It's about me." It *is* a very personal book and every page reveals painful struggle.

There is the struggle to sort a theological stance out of the amalgamation of childhood pietism, seminary liberalism, and post-seminary humanism. There is the struggle to remain in the institutional church, because I know that for me any other base of operation would be a cop-out; yet, there is also a struggle to stay free and courageous enough to bite the hand that feeds me when the institution castrates human dignity with its irrelevant wheel-spinning and its exclusive fraternalism.

This is the story of the struggle of a white family living for the past five years in a black community and being put down and shut out by so many who can't get beyond skin color to personhood. It is the story of an identity crisis brought on by a minority stance for which there was no preparation. It is the story of a white man with no previous exposure to black people serving as pastor of a congregation that is two-thirds black.

This book also holds the struggle of a man who wants to be known by his name and not by his title. It is a plea for individual identity and for the privacy of one's own freely chosen style of life. It also depicts the fears and the pain of a man who is committed to following the Lord and not the bishop, yet knowing all the time that the bishop pays better.

This book *is* about me. But, at the same time, it is very much about you, too. My struggles are a part of the larger battle of man as he searches for his own integrity. I invite you to listen to my story and appropriate it where you can for the living of the days in which you find yourself.

I've been as honest as I am free to be at this point in my life. I've pulled a few punches, but not many. And while the book is a protest of sorts, there is far more hope than despair; far more victory than defeat; far more power than impotence.

I am grateful to Dr. Carlyle Marney, who listened for hours to my struggle and said the story should be told. I am indebted to Forum House for encouraging me to get serious about what I perpetually put off. There are many people portrayed in the book without whom there would be neither struggle nor story. I dare not begin that list, but I would be most negligent if I failed to give thanks and love to the four women in my harem, Margaret Anne, Lisa Anne, Kara Lynn, and Amy Leigh.

Every man has a girl Friday who makes him look good. Mine is Mrs. Nellie Jo Espin, who tirelessly typed pages and pages of thoughts, afterthoughts, and second thoughts. Her typing was errorless, her spirit perfect. Thank you, Nellie Jo.

Phil Barnhart
Atlanta, Georgia
1972

CHAPTER 1

Damned if I do – damned if I don't

"You're a dirty nigger-loving Communist!"

There was a click and the gruff voice was gone. My hands shook and I felt sick at my stomach.

It was just an isolated incident, I thought. I tackled the work piled on my desk and soon felt better.

The phone rang again:

"We don't want you around here, Whitey. Get the hell out!"

I went home that night a man without a country. The whites didn't want me and the blacks didn't need me. I had expected crank calls from the right, but not from the left. I had already tasted rejection from friends and colleagues, but to be rejected so soon by a black man, prominent and professional, was extra hard to swallow. I had only been at East Lake two months and he had never laid eyes on me. What did he know about how I felt and why I had moved into the community? I had been convicted without trial and I didn't like it one bit.

My thoughts went back four months to a country parsonage scene and the cautioning of a district superintendent.

"I'm concerned about your family's safety," he said. "When you go to East Lake, let's sell the parsonage and move you to a nicer community."

I leaned hard on the edge of my worn-out chair. My voice choked. Never before had I disagreed with a district superintendent.

"If you do that, get yourself another boy. I'm not going. You can't love people from a distance."

Now, I wondered. Had he been right? Was my family safe? Was my life in danger? I didn't want to be a martyr, particularly before I'd done anything for which I would be worth shooting.

Another colleague had warned me,

"Barnhart, you're a damn fool!"

"Why?"

"If you take your wife into that community, some nigger will rape her within six weeks."

I argued with vehemence that approached violence. In anger and disgust, I left him. What did he know?

Not only would my family and I be venturing into an unknown land; we were also helplessly watching bridges burn behind us.

One of my parishioners said to me:

"We've had you three years on this circuit. We figured we'd lose you, but we didn't figure we'd lose you to a bunch of niggers."

Another spoke up. "My wife and I had planned to visit you when you left here. Now we won't be comin'."

Several contemporaries cautioned that if I went to East Lake, there would be numerous doors closed to me. A district superintendent told me that I would be hard to place after East Lake and that the longer I stayed, the more difficult it would be.

As I sat in my office with "Get the hell out!" reverberating in my ears, all of these thoughts flooded my mind with a rush of doubt.

Had I acted too hastily? Was the call that I had heard really from God, or did it arise out of my own need for notice and notoriety? Had I taken Margaret Anne, Lisa, and Kara into something for which I would be terribly sorry?

As if all this were not enough, an incident of the previous week returned to haunt me. A terrified boy had come bolting down the driveway.

"Re — Re — Reverend Ba — Ba — Barnhart, co — come quick. My — my brothers are killin' each other."

"Where?"

"O — o — over on your church yard. They — they got knives and Jimmy's c — c — cut."

I dashed across the street and was in the middle of it before I knew what I had done. My diversion gave one combatant a chance to run. Begging and pleading, I followed the other to his house, which he tore apart until he found a shotgun, jammed in two shells, and took off. I pursued him, then gave up and went home.

Soon, the doorbell rang and there was Jimmy, holding his side.

"Please help me. I'm hurt and he's still after me."

I let Jimmy in and watched Margaret Anne patch him up the best she could.

"We've got to get you out of here," I said.

I put him in my car and sped to the other side of town, where I let him out in front of his shanty apartment.

"Go in there, lock the door, and don't come out for anyone."

I was almost home when two youngsters flagged me.

"Reverend Barnhart, George is looking for you. He's gonna kill you for buttin' in."

Had I angered George that much? Was his threat serious? Did he still harbor his grudge? Would he kill me? Should I leave East Lake? Could I still get out gracefully?

Entering my home after the two nasty phone calls, and still thinking of George's threat, I recalled other feelings — positive feelings — of recent months which my fright had momentarily chased away. My strength returned and I knew, for the first of many times to be, that courage is fear that has said its prayers.

Sometimes we're frightened, not by the threatening phone calls or the violent black youths or other external hazards that may come into our lives, but rather by disturbing feelings inside us. It is to your struggles of the inner sort that I want to recommend the power of prayer. Prayer has sustained us these last five years at East Lake. Your doubts and conflicts probably spring from different origins, but the source and strength of prayer is the same for everyone.

This awareness of prayer's power began at our country pastorate as Margaret Anne and I struggled with whether or not to go to East Lake.

We listened a little skeptically as our friend Ken Crossman told us of Gideon's fleece. Gideon, wanting a sign that the Lord would deliver Israel from the hands of the Midianites, put a fleece of wool on the threshing floor and told the Lord, "If there is dew on the fleece alone and it is dry on all the ground, then I shall know thou wilt deliver Israel by my hand as thou hast said." Morning came and it was so. Still wanting to be certain, Gideon put it to the Lord again, "Let it be dry only on the fleece and on all the ground let there be dew." Morning came and it was so.

As Margaret Anne and I stood with Ken under stretching oak trees, he challenged us. "Go on, put the fleece out on East Lake. Ask God for a sign."

"But what kind of sign?" I stalled.

"Go Gideon one better. Don't specify anything. Ask God to put His own sign out."

The three of us formed a circle of commitment. We dared to test God. We even had the audacity to name the date by which we must know. "April twenty-ninth," I said, almost whispering.

Circuit riders have fifth Sundays off, and on the fifth Sunday weekend of April, 1967, we were guests of my confidant and colleague, Jimmy Thompson, for whom I was to preach. Saturday night, Jimmy and I were in the church parlor and I told him of the fleece. We began to pray, as was our custom, and in the middle of my prayer he blurted out, "I know what it is!"

"You what?"

"I know what the fleece is."

"Don't stop."

"Midnight tonight is the deadline?"

"Right."

"The fleece is for Margaret Anne to tell you, unequivocally, that she wants to go to East Lake."

It made sense. I had already decided I wanted to go, but God would have to call Margaret Anne, too. Jimmy and I went to his home and after some chitchat, Margaret Anne and I excused ourselves and went to the guest room. As I got ready for bed, I wondered if anything would happen regarding the sign from God. We had a brief meditation but nothing was said about our dilemma. As I reached for the light switch, Margaret Anne said, "Phil."

"Yes, honey."

"I want to go to East Lake."

I looked at the clock.

It was one minute before midnight.

God's sign had summoned me to East Lake; now, months later, it sustained me. I had become aware of an extra dimension, a supporting power, a believable presence. God opened a door. I went through it and stood in a larger room.

This doesn't mean that doubts have ceased altogether. Recently, someone asked me if I ever felt like quitting. I replied, "How many days are there in the week?" Every year at conference time I especially get itchy feet. I've talked to men in other conferences; once I came close to making a change. I've answered interdenominational church ads from all over the country. I've scanned the local want ads, thinking there must be an easier way to make a living.

You've wanted to run away, too, haven't you? Haven't you thought of turning in flight from that rude boss or impossible customer? Haven't you threatened to get out of the system; away from the institution; far from the rat race? Haven't you thought of skipping out on the little wife — or of leaving the screaming kids for someone else to look after? We all experience times when we want to run from something. But usually we stay.

> "I've been scarred and battered
>   My hopes the wind done scattered.
> Snow has friz' me,
>   Sun has baked me,
> Looks like between 'em they done
>   tried to make me
> Stop laughin', stop lovin', stop livin'
>   But I don't care;
> I'm still here!"

> —Langston Hughes

I'm glad I stayed. It's been hell, but with a whole lot of heaven thrown in. There is unmistakable evidence of a new dimension of power in my life. If I had run away, I might never have stopped running.

True, many days my feet won't even drag, let alone march. In such a time, I plunge into project and program and wheel and deal the day away. At midnight, I'm tired but not sleepy. I'm through work for the day but still treading the mill. I boost myself, promote myself, sell myself until I'm an empty hull of aching bone and tired blood.

Then I pray — out loud, silently, kneeling, standing

up. I don't *talk* about prayer. I *pray*! If there is anything we should stop talking about and get on with, it's prayer.

There was a day when I was forever putting prayer off for a time more appropriate, a place more convenient, a group more conducive. Then I stood with Rosemary in Ira Levin's *Rosemary's Baby* as she said, "If only prayer were still possible! How nice it would be to hold a crucifix again and have God's ear."

Yes, I remember months on end when I couldn't pray. The practice of prayer had slipped away. I prayed only when someone made me. I prayed professionally. I felt guilty, lonely, impotent.

"Lord, teach me to pray!" I cried. I went to prayer seminars only to find that the experts didn't practice prayer, they discussed it. I wanted to *do* it.

We are not called to analyze prayer nor even to understand it. It is not something at which you are "proficient" or "effective." Prayer is something at which *you* are *yourself*. It is not something you organize and calculate. It's something you plunge into out of your gut from a notion of need and a perspective of praise. When you really come in prayer, you come naked, exposed, vulnerable, and just empty enough to be filled.

Now I pray all the time, it seems. Prayer is the stance in which I face every day. Prayer gives me courage to hear the threats and not fall apart. Prayer breaks open the light when the aura of hopelessness breeds only darkness and futility. (Later in these pages I will describe the experiences that led to this new zeal for prayer.)

I went to East Lake convinced that God had called

me there.

I've stayed because the call remains.

The strength I feel in the face of danger, frustration, loneliness continues to be a "fleece" confirming my decision and upholding me in it. The new dimension of power that I have proves this is where God wants me to be.

There are other signs.

For example, the children who are taught through our tutorial programs and summer school.

I was leaning over a ten-year-old, pressing him to add a column of figures. I checked his paper and announced, "You got it right."

"I did?"

"Yes, you did."

"Gee, Reverend Barnhart, I have a brain, don't I?"

"Yes, you certainly do!"

There was the twenty-year-old dropout, just released from jail, where I had visited her several times. We sat together in our study hall working on multiplication tables in preparation for her equivalency exam.

"I'm just too old to learn this stuff."

"That's crazy talk, and I don't want to hear any more of it."

"But I've never done anything right."

"Not a word of truth in that. Do you remember what you told me in jail?"

"That I wanted to be somebody?"

"Yes, and what did I tell you?"

"That I was already somebody."

"You are! Now pick up that pencil and prove it."

There have been other confirmations. Mothers having no milk for their babies have been supplied. School kids with no coats for their backs have been clothed. Skeptics who had taken their talents from the church have brought them back. The poverty-stricken have been turned on to Jesus Christ because of a church that cares. We believe in compassion — *your* pain in *our* heart — and we practice what we preach.

I see a rising tide of care and concern among churches across this country and I have hope. Five years ago, I was a classic under-thirty, fed-up cynic on his way out of the ministry. Now I'm over thirty, and I'm still a cynic — still fed up enough to avoid complacency and cowardice — but I'm not on the way out of the ministry. I have a vision of what the church will do, because I have seen what she has done and is doing.

A major reason I stay in the ministry is that the church has shown me, in the last few years, that she is willing to struggle. God speaks to and through a church that is willing to stay on the case and let it all hang out. God acted by way of the cross of Jesus, and today He acts by way of the cross the church bears when she is willing to die in order to live. If I believe in the gospel of the cross, then it is my duty to stay within the church and make my dissatisfactions felt through the crucible of change, confusion, and death.

Struggle on, O Church of Christ! Struggle with the diversity of your membership all the way from Cecil Williams to George Wallace. Struggle with the myriad of theological positions — pietist, secularist, fundamentalist, humanist. Struggle with the demands of blacks, women,

Chicanos, seminarians, and the gay liberation front. (As long as there's caucus, there'll be no carcass.) Struggle with structure. Struggle with new music and new forms of worship. Struggle with war in Vietnam, church investments in South Africa, and abortion in New York City.

Struggle on, O Church of Christ! Struggle against status quo, tired tradition, and perfunctory protocol.

As long as the church is in honest and vulnerable struggle, I plan to remain on board the ship. I may be damned if I do and damned if I don't, but I'm staying.

CHAPTER 2

From a minority stance

When we moved into the East Lake community, I was determined to demonstrate that I really cared. At the first siren, I was off and running. I turned up at every accident, every fire, every shooting. But somehow my message of caring didn't get through.

During my second week at East Lake, I walked up some stairs and knocked on a door.

"What do you want?"

"I understand your grandmother is dying."

"What's it to you?"

"I want to help, if I can."

"No way, man."

The door swung shut again.

That was rather typical in those early days. It was rough experience, but I wouldn't trade it for any high steeple. It's in this way that I've begun to discover who I am. The most significant thing about my ministry is what has happened to me — inside myself!

It began because for the first time in my life, I had to

operate from a minority stance. All my years, I had functioned from a majority position.

I was born and raised middle class and I'll probably die middle class. I am white, which means that I'm a part of an eighty percent racial majority in this country. I am Protestant and belong to one of the largest denominations. To strengthen my credentials, I have college degrees.

Without being aware of it, I had let these assertive forces dictate my life style. I had let them rob me of the joy of knowing my own identity and being my own man.

This suddenly changed when I moved into a black community and became a minority figure. My whiteness caused me to stick out like a sore thumb, making me easy prey for anger, hostility, blank grunts, and cold stares. Some people looked through me as if I didn't exist.

Lisa and I were out walking when three young men came along.

"Hello there," I said.

There was no reply.

"How are you?"

Still nothing as they went on down the street, chomping on their toothpicks and snapping their fingers.

"Are they mad at us, daddy?"

"I don't think so."

"But they didn't talk to me."

"We'll see them again, honey. Maybe they'll talk then."

This group didn't talk to Lisa that time, but she soon

became my ambassador. She could make people speak to her. She sparkled her blue eyes, flashed that generous smile, and threw up her little hand. Even the most hostile warmed a bit.

Every member of my family has helped to establish credibility in a community where we were promptly put down. Their attitudes and actions have been natural, with no hints of superiority and no attempts to manipulate.

Two of my daughters have spent most of their lives in East Lake, and the third daughter has spent all of her life there. They know nothing else. Lisa was two when we moved in and she never missed a step in her excitable, aggressive style. She made people speak to her whether they wanted to or not. Kara was just a few months old when we moved and, though she is far more reticent than Lisa, her large, moist, brown eyes became magnets that even the most suspicious could not resist. Amy was born after two years at East Lake, and with her we had another freewheeling, uninhibited ambassador whose busy cadence and bright smile said "I love you" to everyone.

The mother of these three girls is my better two-thirds and a helpmate unexcelled. Margaret Anne was raised in a tolerant home where love and affection were freely expressed with no hint of embarrassment or reluctance. She expressed this love in our new community with a grace that was both winsome and natural. She continued to do what she had always done, but it was a breath of fresh air for many who were accustomed to either a blatant bigotry or a phony paternalism.

When we first moved to East Lake, I knew I must meet the youth, so I found a basketball, donned my tennis shoes, and went to the playground courts. I stood there, by myself, for days.

"Do you wanna' let whitey play?"

"Aw, he's too old and fat."

"Come on, he's been here all week."

"Okay."

"Hey, you, wanna' play some?"

It was a small but heartening beginning.

In five years, there have been over 70 young men in our programs who were first met in just this way. Introductions came hard. I was never punched in the nose, although I was cursed a few times. Mostly, I was ignored. I was white and that's all they needed to know about me. It said everything.

My middle-class status also made me an easy target for a put-down. People thought I was born with a silver spoon in my mouth. Many assumed I was a slave to materialism and would do anything to improve my bank statement, no matter whose toes I stepped on. They assumed that I found meaning only through possessions and could have no soul.

Because of my WASP image, most assumed I had no use for anybody outside my own cathedral. I was expected to live behind stained glass and confine my services to a privileged few. When someone pointed to my having elected to live in the community, it was excused in various ways.

"He's writing a book."

"It's a research project and we're the guinea pigs again."

"He's here to make it look good so the big shots can say they tried."

"They just want us to join so they can pass whitey's debt on to us."

My formal education also worked a handicap. Some feared that my education would give me some kind of occult mastery over them which I would use to manipulate, control, and exploit.

"You been to college?"

"Yes."

"How long?"

"Seven years in all."

"I guess you think you're some kind of intellectual, don't you?"

"No, I don't think I'm an intellectual. But I think I'm intelligent, just as you are intelligent."

There were a lot of assumptions about me, my family, and the few whites who remained in the church. Many of the blacks in the community made themselves foolish by swallowing myth and assuming that everything derives from color. I played the fool by getting uptight and offended. I was wearing my feelings on my sleeve.

However, without knowing it, we did each other a big favor. My presence forced many blacks to deal with a white man as a resident — neighbor — minister — and, eventually, as a person. Their favor to me was making me deal with myself. Their mistrust of my trimmings of race, class, and status forced me to ask the primal question, "Who am I?"

I thought of how Viktor Frankl must have felt when his Auschwitz captors took away his precious manuscript and his clothes, sent his family to the gas room, shaved every hair on his body, and sent him to the shower.

"While we were waiting for the shower,
our nakedness was brought home to us;
we really had nothing except our bare bodies—
even minus hair; all we possessed, literally,
was our naked existence."

Frankl asked the primal question, "Who am I?" He searched for his "who-ness."

The situation that generated my awareness was not nearly so dramatic, but the experience was just as real to me. Suddenly, those images on which I depended became thorns and thistles. Where once my status symbols had given me an edge in this world, now they were appendages of disability.

As I discovered the valuelessness of these symbols, I felt naked and exposed — first to myself, then to others. I was forced to look for the real person hidden under the vestments of race, economics, and religion. I began to uncover the "I" of my existence. The process was agonizing, but the result was sheer joy. It felt like warm, moist wind in my face to be honest about my own self. I had a whole host of new feelings.

One of these was the joy of freedom. I no longer had to be concerned about how a white, middle-class, religious person should act. I acted like myself. The first months at East Lake, the criterion for my every statement was, "How will this sound to a black man, coming from a white man?" Later, I saw that this was phony and I spoke freely from a newly discovered identity.

An identity struggle is a springboard for all of us, isn't it? Each man is a phony at some point; he carefully calculates his remarks and weighs every word on the basis of who is listening. For instance, in front of their minister, most laymen talk a different talk and walk a different walk. I was pastor to a congregation whose members threw a lot of parties. I could always tell which parties were wet and which were dry: I wasn't invited to the wet parties! How discriminating for them not to give me a choice! How hypocritical of those people who had one mask for their friends and another for their pastor! I want to be invited to *all* of your parties! I like parties! You just might like me at them!

We all play games, but after I had spent a while in the crucible of crisis, many of the games that I had formerly played faded away. I quit going to the "right" places to be seen by the "right" people in an effort to ride the ecclesiastical escalator. I escaped the bag of doing what "preachers" are supposed to do; going where "preachers" are supposed to go; saying what "preachers" are supposed to say.

"Why, that's not what a preacher should say."

"What do you mean?"

"You know — it just doesn't sound like a preacher."

"Maybe not, but it sounds like Phil."

I acquired a certain meaningful audacity that was new to me. For the first time, I understood what Tillich meant:

"Courage is self-affirmation 'in spite of,'
that is in spite of that which tends to prevent
the self from affirming itself."

As I discovered my "I," I began, obviously and with little premeditation, to communicate the personal pronoun. When I did, things began to happen.

As I became more authentic, the black people saw me as a little less white and little more Phil. The stereotypes receded and doors began to open. People started inviting me into their homes, first with a reluctant curiosity, then with a warm openness.

People began to hear the Word preached on Sunday mornings where, earlier, they had only heard the white race in a long robe behind a wooden desk. Not being black, I have neither the rhythm nor cadence of good black preaching. The homiletical road has been one of the roughest roads I've had to travel at East Lake Church, but the Holy Spirit is a good translator. He speaks God's message, often in spite of the messenger. One of my most prized possessions is this letter:

Dear Rev. Barnhart,

Because East Lake is more convenient for me, I have been attending worship services there for some time now.

Frankly speaking, I have had great difficulty getting used to you as the preacher.

For months I could only hear a white man and remember what white men have done to me and my family.

I thought you would want to know, that today I heard God speak.

Sincerely,
Jonathan Henson

There are many persons with less patience and generosity. Some dropped in because of curiosity and dropped out because the music didn't rock and the preacher didn't shout. Others just couldn't cut it with a white man in the pulpit. A government employee told me that he liked what I had to say and that my style wasn't bad — but I was still white. He left and took his wife with him.

A young scientist wouldn't come near a worship service. I went to him. We spent two hours in animated conversation. We were really rappin'. Then he said:

"You make sense."

"I hope I do."

"I like you."

"That's a compliment."

"But I don't trust you."

"Why not?"

"One simple reason. You're white."

What do you say to a person when he confronts you like that?

Although some turned me off, many were willing to stay on, hoping — maybe knowing — that ultimately God would break His bread.

The perseverance of these faithful people enabled God to continue what he had begun in my gut. The struggle to know myself went on. Affirmations came in and I claimed each one with relish.

When the word of Martin Luther King's assassination came, I was chaperoning a hundred teenagers at a dance in our fellowship hall. They were all black — I was white. I saw myself as an obvious target for their hurt and anger. I was sympathetic with their tears, but I was relieved when they went home.

When Margaret Anne heard the news, she came to the church to give me support. We talked and prayed, and then I asked her to go home to the children, which she did.

I telephoned the radio stations and asked them to announce that our sanctuary would be open all night for prayer. Minutes later, the phone rang.

"I hear the church is open all night."

"Yes, it is."

"Who's going to stay there?"

"I am."

"Alone?"

"Yes."

"No, you're not. I'll be right over."

Soon a tall black man, who later was to become our lay leader, was by my side.

All night long, people poured in to pray and to talk.

"What will happen to what we've started here at East Lake Church?"

"I don't know."

"It won't be as easy now."

"That's certain."

"But, Reverend, we'll make it!"

In a time like that, this was a real affirmation!

As time passed, word of my pastoral ministry rippled out. A young couple whom I didn't know came in for premarital counsel; they had heard that I spent time with couples but didn't have my hand out for an honorarium. An unwed couple asked me to bury their infant child; I had helped this young lady's little brother with his homework, and Margaret Anne had sewn up his britches a time or two.

A man who was caught in a family crisis had told me that he joined East Lake solely to get his wife off his back. Now we were having conversations and he had come to accept me as both pastor and friend. A janitor told me I was the first white man he had ever trusted. An assembly-line worker said he had always put down the white race as scheming and cruel, but since we had become friends, he could no longer feel this way.

For a long time, I was always between a rock and a hard place — damned if I did and damned if I didn't. The whites didn't want me and the blacks didn't need me. I anticipated and accepted white ostracism. Now, the people in my new community had begun to pick up what I had sought so desperately to communicate. I was no longer automatically put down because of my white skin.

For the first time, I'm able to see inside myself. I am learning to let the other fellow see me naked and exposed. Relationships ripen and community is celebrated.

Perhaps the most rewarding evidence of acceptance came during a heated argument with one of the church leaders over a new direction for East Lake Church. The discussion turned to fiery debate.

During an outburst I began laughing.

"What's so funny?" he demanded.

"Do you know what has just happened?"

"I'm not sure."

"You and I have walked on eggs for months and now we're in a knock-down, drag-out argument without a single racial connotation. You're mad at me and I'm mad as you — as Leroy and Phil, not as black and white."

He smiled. "Today our relationship has reached a high level," he said. So it had.

He may have thought I was an s.o.b., but not a *white* s.o.b. That's progress.

Thank you, Lord. Thank you so much.

CHAPTER 3

Hardening of the categories

We were caught up in a spirit of comradeship. We turned the corner with my stride matching his. We bumped into one of his friends, and my companion began laying it on thick. He told how involved I was, that I served an integrated church, and on and on. Then he said, "Joe, I want you to meet —" He stopped cold and his expression told on him. He had forgotten my name! But he recovered quickly. "Oh, well, you know how it is," he said. "White people all look alike."

All my life I had heard that black people all look alike — you can't tell Leroy from Lucius, James from Willie. I hadn't been in the East Lake community six weeks until I learned that blacks say the same thing about whites. You can't tell Barnhart from Bankston — they all look alike.

We are hung up on color; we see only a blob of black or a blob of white. Howard Thurman, in *Luminous Darkness*, writes, "The burden of being black and the burden of being white is so heavy that it is rare in our society to experience oneself as a human being."

This attitude which afflicts our world applies to more than a black-white issue. The rich look down their noses at the poor, and the poor look down their noses at the rich. The Occidentals and the Orientals regard each other categorically. Men and women try to shove each other into neat little pigeonholes. Within the black race, the light-skinned and the dark-skinned have at it. The Methodists have every Baptist figured out, and the Baptists return tit for tat. The secularists presume to know what the pietists will do in every situation, and the pietists the same. Ministers lump laymen all into one pile, and laymen "know how preachers are."

I wish people wouldn't use the word "they" in a derogatory sense. It ostracizes, it discriminates, it pushes a man into the corner of category where all his attitudes are presupposed and all his actions prejudged. It puts him in a box with a final label on it, and then it no longer listens to what he has to say but instead comments, "Well, you know how *they* are."

"They" is an ugly word for it robs man of a most precious treasure — his individualism. If you're from South Georgia, "they" says you are a redneck and you hate blacks. If you are a black man with an "afro" and a beard, you are a smart-alec militant. If your hair is long, you are a no-good pot-smoker, or if you carry a picket sign, you are a "commie." "They" says all this, then leans back to remark, "Well, *they* are all alike, you know."

Society is dying of *hardening of the categories*. You know about hardening of the *arteries* — the arteries fill with sludge and grow brittle, impeding blood flow and often causing disability or death. Well, society is dying of hardening of the *categories*, and the church is encouraging the disease.

The style and stance of Christians facing the future must be to tell it like it is, but first they must see it like it is. One obvious symptom of our hardening categories is the flight of the church and her people to the suburbs. We have made Moses' exodus look like a trickle. See how they run!

Postwar revivalism, which was an awakening of questionable value, saw a building boom. Church architecture became a most lucrative field, and many architects did nothing else. Then, we were constructing buildings. Now, we are closing buildings because the "new" people don't fit into our category.

I'm thinking of a church that our conference closed not long ago. It was an adequate facility with a large sanctuary that was quite appropriate to praise God, Father of all blessings. This church building had seen some great days when decisions were made, lives changed, identities discovered. It had once been a stronghold of the faith, ringing out the name of Jesus with clarity and conviction. This church had once been captivated by a servant theology and had knelt with basin and towel.

Then, the color of the feet changed. The church looked down, dropped its towel, fell sprawling over its basin, clambered to its feet, sold its building, and ran out to find the security of sameness. This church swallowed the American myth — on which it will yet choke.

It believed those ridiculous put-downs that begin with "they." It fell victim to that plague of prejudice which Marney defines as "a vicious kind of mental slant pushed up out of your culture that makes up your mind for you before you think."

When will contemporary Christians think for themselves and get out of granddaddy's rut? We really put our lack of intelligence on display when we blindly imitate the past with no concern for what we know to be true in the present. It is more than a church building that we sell — we sell our integrity, our discipleship, maybe even our soul.

East Lake Church came close to doing just that. Her people watched as church after church ran after the pied piper of prejudice. A church only three miles away sold to a black congregation. A church one and one-half miles away did the same. A church less than a mile away sold a magnificent edifice — pipe organ and all — to the Atlanta Board of Education for use as an elementary school. It was bad enough to remove the church from the community; it was worse still to accommodate a board of education which should have built a new school, in the first place.

The several hundred members of East Lake Church watched all this and decided to follow suit. In the spring of 1967 the congregation voted to close and sell to anyone who would buy. It looked as though the exodus had swallowed another victim.

But God would not be turned from His purpose for East Lake. Several of the people began to discuss a ministry to the community. They were joined by the pastor (my predecessor) and the district superintendent. The conference agreed to help subsidize a large building indebtedness. A survey was taken to solicit support from the membership. Fifty people pledged to stay and serve.

In July, 1967, Margaret Anne and I and our two daughters joined these fifty who were committed to rescuing their church from hardening of the categories. The rebirth has been a breath of fresh air for an institution which had for a long time been content merely to serve tea to itself.

The East Lake story is one of struggle and suffering for those who forsook family and friends to put on the full armor of God. It is the story of frustration and failure for those whose intentions were admirable but couldn't cut the mustard and fell by the wayside.

The East Lake story is a story of help and hope for unwed mothers who have turned to Christ's people for support and counsel; of practical assistance for the hungry and underclothed who have received food from our pantry shelf and coats from our clothing room; of a future assured for youngsters because they now can read, thanks to our dedicated tutors.

One chapter of the East Lake story relates the encouragement and challenge provided a young man who once had no one in his corner and now has a whole family to recommend him. Another chapter describes how a community which once had no institution to rally around has been given the soul to keep on keepin' on and the guts to resist becoming another slum of junk cars and king rats.

Because of East Lake, my young friend won't end up

in prison now; he has better things to do. Several school dropouts study math, science, and English at East Lake Church; they will soon get their high school degree. Others learn typing skills that will enable them to command a better job. Ladies are taught to sew; their wardrobe is increased and their dollars saved.

The East Lake story is one of what can happen when God puts into a few hands the pebbles of David. It is the story of the enthusiasm of Peter, the determination of Paul, and the perseverance of Job. It is a story of God's power turned loose in our lives to meet our faith in deeds of love and service. The East Lake story is the story of a church that is both a haven in which to rest and a harbor from which to sail.

We, too, have had our category problems. Although we are headed in the right direction, we have a long way to go.

He was black and he said, "You're letting the riffraff in the church."

"Pardon me?"

"These dirty little snotty-nose kids around here."

"They're God's children."

"I just left an all-black church because of this. I thought I was coming to better."

"Would you please walk outside with me for a minute?"

"Sure."

We faced the sign in front of the church building. "What does it say this church is?"

"A church for all people."

"What does that mean?"

"This is a place where black and white people can worship and work together."

"Yes — but not that only. It's a church for *all* people, and that includes little snotty-nose kids."

The easiest thing for me to do is to call the hand of categorization when it's black or white. It has been harder for me to call it wherever I see it.

A delegation of youth visited me. They were all black.

"We want to talk with you about our Sunday School class."

"Okay, I'm all ears."

"It's hard to say —"

"Just push it. It'll come."

"Well — we don't want that yellow man teaching our class."

"Do you know what you just said?"

"What do you mean?"

"You just said about Ching the same thing that people have said about you for over three hundred years."

"Oh."

A major hurdle for some people has been the baptism of infants of unwed mothers. One Sunday, a father was also present. I made no special fuss over the names, but they were obviously different.

The next morning I was visited by a white lady.

"I don't like what you did yesterday."

"I'm not sure I follow you."

"You know — baptizing that illegitimate child."

"I'm not sure what *illegitimate* is. She's a child of God."

"You should have done it in your office."

"But baptism is a community sacrament."

"Well, maybe you're right. But I'm not used to it."

"It's new to me, too."

"It is?"

"Of course. But it's what God wants us to do!"

At East Lake, the categories aren't so starkly defined as they once were. We are learning to relate to people as *who* they are and not *what* they are.

For a while, my oldest daughter was so unaware of categories, she didn't even know what color she was. When she was four, I asked her,

"What color is your hair?"

"Blond."

"That's right. What color are your eyes?"

"Blue."

"That's right. What color is your skin?"

"Black."

For the most part, Lisa had associated with black children and so she thought she looked like everyone else. Later, when she was in the first grade and had learned there were at least two colors, she told her teacher that it didn't make any difference what color you are, we are all God's children. The teacher congratulated us for telling Lisa this. We replied, "We've never said a word; we didn't have to. It's been a way of life for her." When children are raised without reference to categories, "it ain't no big thing."

Many people have asked me when I became convinced that God's children can all get together. I cannot locate the realization in terms of time and space. Many factors have contributed.

I believed what they said in seminary. It turned me on to hear my young, intelligent professors speak so passionately of justice for everyone. We were in the early Sixties then, and every week was punctuated with sit-ins, sleep-ins, and pray-ins. The news media were filled with the exploits of Martin Luther King, Jr., and our classrooms were full of opinions and presentations concerning his ethic, theology, and influence. It was a great time for brotherhood. Almost every man who went through seminary in those days came out with a thirst for unity and equality.

I began to take my New Testament seriously. It ceased to be nice little stories about what God *used* to do and became a contemporary gospel relevant to all that hit the headlines. The Good Samaritan story became my sword and saber, and Jesus' life style became one to imitate rather than to worship.

The influence of my friends also stirred me to challenge the categories. The senior minister for whom I worked for two years took some mighty unpopular stands in a very conservative setting and taught me that no price is too high to pay for personal integrity. The young people in that same church kept me honest through their idealism and enthusiasm. My wife and children inspire me by living the sermons I preach.

These are all reasons why I am committed to resist categories and remain open to every possible human encounter. However, the main reason comes out of my upbringing.

One day, Martin Luther King, Sr., was preaching at East Lake Church. While we waited for the time to begin the service, he looked out over the congregation and turned to me.

"Where did you get the notion that something like this would work?"

"I'm not sure. I guess I got it from my mother." That's the origin of much of my theology of justice and inclusiveness. I hadn't realized it until then. I sat down and wrote Mom a letter.

> Dear Mom,
>
> A mother gives a child many things and you are no exception.
>
> You gave a sense of physical security and, at the same time, a proper sense of values. You gave a strict standard of morality and, yet, a freedom that allowed growth and eliminated many of the traditional hang-ups. You gave a sensitivity for the spiritual and, at the same time, the deliverance from the agony of living life as a sour-faced saint.
>
> Perhaps the greatest gift I have from you is an appreciation of people as persons. Thank you that I never heard you use the word "nigger" or "wop" or "spic." Thank you that my friends — Sam Kandis, Joe Tatich, and Neal Goodman — were not introduced to me as the Greek, the Russian, and the Jew but as Sam, Joe, and Neal.
>
> Thank you that I never learned the socio-economic strata of American life in my home.

I never knew what lower, middle, and upper class meant.

Thank you that what many struggle with — the acceptance of those different than they — has always been sort of second nature to me.

What greater gift could a mother give her son than this?

> I love you.
> Phillip

Without knowing it, my mother prepared the way for my pastorate at East Lake Church. Without what she taught (more in deed than in word), I wouldn't have lasted a week.

The most exciting worship service I have ever been a part of was one not long ago at East Lake. As they came to the rail, I studied them.

There was a hard-working domestic, black, with hands splintered from scrubbing white folks' floors. There was a Ph.D. seminary professor of mine. There was a dashiki-clad youth with an "afro" comb stuck in his high hair. There was a middle-class white man who has stayed with us through thick and thin.

There was a young, bearded, white union worker, dressed in dungarees and sneakers. There was an Oriental student. There was a poor white lady from the "projects" who knows she belongs with us. There was a district superintendent's wife who broke precedent by affiliating with East Lake Church.

They were all these different persons . . . but first they were children of God. I'm just fundamental enough to believe that every man, woman, and child for whom Christ died is my brother and sister. I thank God I'm in a church where we practice what I preach.

I can best close this chapter by sharing with you a prayer we use frequently. It is from *Ventures in Worship*, edited by David James Randolph for the Commission on Worship of The United Methodist Church:

"Lord, it is so difficult today to accept your love and to realize its importance. We are so tossed about by ideologies and accusations. If we are white and low income, we are said to be unorganized and helpless. If we are black and low income, we are said to be crippled with a low self-image and family disintegration.

"If we are white and middle class, we are called either bigots or paternalistic liberals. If we are black and middle class, we are thought of as traitors to the cause. If we are white and really involved, we are told to move back and keep quiet. If we are black and really involved, we are called neo-racists and threats to public order.

"There is no way of existing without being declared guilty. We are not asking you to help us cover up the truth about ourselves. We don't want to become unconscious of our hang-ups, of our need for healing. What we want, Lord, like cool water flowing into us on a hot day, is to believe and feel that you love us now.

"If we can love ourselves now as your creation, your children, your beloved, maybe we can act from the inside with freedom. Don't let our own beauty depend upon declaring others ugly. Help us to feel good about ourselves, who we are, our living, our dying. If you will help us, we can begin to love each other. Amen."

CHAPTER 4

Don't call me preacher

It's my instinct for individualism that makes me fight for my identity as a unique person. I resist categories because they assume everything. No man can be packaged and labeled automatically.

Racial labels conclude every man who is of a particular hue behaves like every other man of that color. Geographical labels listen for an accent, then predict actions and attitudes. People even categorize us because we are short people or tall people.

Professional labels are as cruelly restricting. He's a doctor, so what would he know about raising cows? He's a janitor, so he couldn't like classical music. Why, he's a jock, and jocks don't appreciate art. She's a school teacher, so all that she knows about is children. *And you know how preachers are!*

Don't call me Preacher! Don't call me Preacher, damn it! Forcing me into this category chokes my style, stifles my creativity, and drastically threatens my self-image.

Don't call me Preacher! I have a name!

A close friend is a doctor, but I can't lump him with Kildare and Casey. He has a name! Another friend is an automobile dealer. He would vomit if I categorized him with the carnival car hustlers on TV. He has a name!

My name is not "Preacher"! My name is Phil Barnhart.

If people are to relate to me as a person, they have to know what it means to be Phil Barnhart.

Being Phil Barnhart means being the first of two sons in a family where Mom called the shots because Daddy was usually drunk. It means I received masculine traits from a feminine source and feminine traits from a masculine source. It means I've had difficulty relating to women who are strong and decisive because they remind me of a father who was weak and vacillating. I spent 30 years rejecting the qualities that my father gave me — some of them good qualities — because I considered the source invalid.

To be Phil Barnhart means being raised in a home where tolerance was taught by one parent and prejudice taught by the other. One day, when I was ten, Daddy came in from his job as a state prison guard. I watched with cowboy curiosity as he unsheathed his revolver and put it on the dresser. He tossed his handcuffs alongside the gun and took a short, black object from his hip pocket.

"What's that?"

"That's a blackjack."

"What's it made out of?"

"Leather and lead."

"Let me feel it."

"It's hard and heavy."

"What do you use it for?"

"Today I beat two niggers with it."

To be Phil Barnhart means being raised in a small town where everybody knew everybody else. I spent some very embarrassing moments when Daddy's name was listed in the *Moundsville Daily Echo* as being arrested for drunk driving. I also spent some very proud moments in Forbes Field rooting for the Pirates and sitting by a father who knew everything about baseball. It meant being alone a lot because Mom was supporting the family, and yet it meant being grateful that she could.

To be Phil Barnhart means being nurtured in a church where the members constantly fought for power and where ministers were run off in rapid succession. One was booted because he smoked a pipe, another because his wife didn't dress right, still another because he hunted rabbits. It means thinking religion is rules and regulations, yet being confused over whose rules to follow.

To be Phil Barnhart means spending 18 years in an all-white vacuum. I never knew a black person until I went off to college. I was never in a black person's home until, at age 29, I moved into the East Lake community.

I remember sitting on a stool in my favorite ice cream establishment and ordering a marshmallow sundae for my Saturday night treat. I was eight and very proud of the way I could read. There was a sign up on the mirror and I began to read it aloud.

"We only serve members of the —. Daddy, what does c-a-u-c-a-s-i-a-n spell?"

"Caucasian," he replied.

"What does cau-caucasian mean?"

"It means being white."

I quickly looked at myself in the mirror. Yes, I was white. I was so glad! If I'd been black, there would have been no marshmallow sundae.

To be Phil Barnhart means working after school and on Saturdays at a men's clothing store from age 13 to age 18. It means wearing the latest fashions to advertise the goods to the high school students. That was during the pastel craze, and I had chartreuse shirts, heliotrope sweaters, and pink slacks. (Later, when I took a pastoral appointment, I thought I had to dress like a preacher and so I traded my pastels for blacks, greys, and browns. I not only lost my color, but a little of myself, as well. Now I know better. I dress according to my own private sense of style. It may not be ministerial, but it's me.)

To be Phil Barnhart means going to college because Mom made me go, then loving every minute of it. It means working at a steel mill during the summers, developing a great appetite, monstrous blisters, and a keen appreciation for the man who earns his living by the sweat of his brow. It means returning to college for fraternity beer parties, cute little coeds, and an automobile all my own. It means thinking immodestly that I was a BMOC (Big Man on Campus), yet actually gaining self-confidence and leadership qualities that would mean much as I followed the light God gave me.

"My child, continue your knowledge,
Go to college and stay there 'till you're through,
If they can make penicillin from moldy cheese,

They can make somethin' out of you."

— Nipsy Russell

To be Phil Barnhart means getting married the day after graduation to one of those cute little coeds. It means nearly 13 years of a marriage full of both splendor and splinters. It means a wife who gets better, not older. A cliché, but I mean it. Margaret Anne has shared all there was to endure in a hostile community where she and her children were ignored or insulted because they were white. She has stuck to her commitment when the rapes and murders all around her would have driven most women to the safety of suburbia. She has watched her children go to schools where they stuck out like a sore thumb. One year, Lisa was the only white in a kindergarten of more than 100 children. The next year, Kara was the pet whitey. Margaret Anne has experienced all of this and has kept smiling. A smile is her trademark and it's as real as she is.

To be Phil Barnhart means much more, but just say it means I am me. I am an individual. I am unique, different, peculiar. When God made me, he threw the mold away. There's no one like me on the face of the earth, so don't call me Preacher!

My little Lisa understands this. She knows preacher is not all there is. One evening, I was sitting in the den when she answered the back door. I overheard the conversation.

"Is Preacher here?"

"No, he's not."

"But his car is in the driveway."

"The Preacher's not here."

"Is Reverend Barnhart here?"

"No, he's over at the church."

"Is your Daddy here?"

"Yes, Daddy's here!"

Being thought of only as Preacher robs a man of his individualism, but there are other travesties that it commits. It can imply that preaching on Sunday is all you do . . . you work one day a week. There are many people who firmly believe that's all we do. This is particularly true in a black community where many ministers are only preachers. Most of the black ministers I know don't live in the community where their church is, keep no office hours, and have an unlisted telephone number. They motor in once a week to stir up the saints and carry away the dollars. Maybe they deserve to be labeled Preacher. But don't call *me* Preacher!

Let me share a bit of humor with you.

"The pastor teaches, though he must solicit his own classes. He heals, though without pills or knife. He is sometimes a lawyer, often a social worker, something of an editor, a bit of a philosopher and entertainer; a salesman; a decorative piece for public functions, and he is supposed to be a scholar. He visits the sick, marries people, buries the dead, labors to console those who sorrow and to admonish those who sin, and tries to stay sweet when chided for not doing his duty. He plans programs, appoints committees when he can get them; spends considerable time in keeping people out of each other's hair; between times he prepares a sermon and preaches it on Sunday to those who don't happen to have any other engagement. Then on Monday he smiles when some jovial chap roars, 'What a job — one day a week!' " (Anonymous)

Being considered a preacher means people relate to you out of function. When people think of you as banker, they don't think of you in terms of your personhood — they think in terms of what you do for them. When they call you lawyer, your value to them comes out of your doing, not your being.

"Hey boy! What can you do?"
One hundred per cent way to destroy
any possibility
of meeting
anyone.
I don't care who you are —
what can you do?
Can you be of
USE
to me? If so,
hang around."

— Earnest Larsen

When people can't think of me except as Preacher, I sense they are mainly interested in what I can do for them. Can I inspire them on Sunday? Can I meet with their committee on Monday? Can I counsel with them on Tuesday? Can I pray for them on Wednesday? Can I speak at their club on Thursday? Can I get their son out of jail on Friday?

"We need someone to say the blessing at the Lions Club banquet — call the Preacher."

"We can't begin the football game without a prayer — call the Preacher."

"Our parents are coming from Ohio and they are very religious — call the Preacher."

"We ought to have a church represented on that board of directors — call the Preacher."

I cannot live the full life if people see me only as a product or service. I must have friends who love me even when I can't perform for them — even when my friendship is a liability.

In the spring of 1971, I hit a low spot in my tenure at East Lake Church. I went into a serious depression which I couldn't shake. The time came to put out our biweekly newsletter, for which I write a column. I wrote what I felt. Here's my column:

> It may be more blessed to give than to receive but he who only gives soon runs out of soap. The shepherd may feed the sheep, but someone has to feed the shepherd.
>
> The professional who serves others — the doctor, the minister, the social worker — gives of his time, talent, training to all who dial the phone and pound the door. He is committed to the welfare of his constituents and leaves no stone unturned to see they get what's coming to them. And, yet, he hurts and cries inside because he is so alone; so cut off. He is with hundreds of people every week and yet his life is a desert.
>
> Why? Because he needs gifts, too. He needs someone to listen to his problems once in awhile — to encourage him on to the next step — to hear what he is really saying. He has

given all of himself he has to offer for a while and he falters as if he can't go on.

He could make the next step and then some — maybe even move a mountain or two — if people would accept him as he is and not as they've read he should be. He could travel far if there came his way just a little real appreciation; an occasional sincere compliment; the acknowledgement that he needs love and support like everybody else.

But, he's taken for granted. He helps someone and they want to know why not sooner and why not more. He lets the stops out year after year and people assume he'll go on forever. He walks the second mile and they say he's just doing his job — his duty — that's what we pay him for.

He stops — gives up — quits. Then, they praise what he used to do. Then, they remember how much he once helped. But — saddest of sadness — it's too late.

I was weary of functioning in order to have an identity. I desperately cried out for more. My people heard me. They were warm. They were concerned. Mostly, they were shocked.

"We didn't dream you ever felt like that," they said. "You always have a smile. You always seem on top of things."

My confession left me extremely vulnerable, but that's okay. I *am* vulnerable. That's the real me.

That introduces another travesty committed by the Preacher label. Some people assume you are some kind of paragon of virtue. They put you on a pedestal and tack on a tag: "Preacher."

We were in a group where the format was to be honest. I was. I let it all hang out. I spilled my guts all over the floor. I don't know if I ever will again.

He said, "Do you really feel that way?"

"I surely do."

"Are you certain?"

"Yes, why are you so shocked?"

"Well, you're not *supposed* to feel that way."

"Why not?"

" 'Cause you're a preacher."

Preachers are people. They're not a third sex. Yes, they're obligated to set an example, but not a perfect one. (We're all obligated to set examples, aren't we?)

Nobody's perfect, not even preachers. We play the fool when we equate being a Christian with being perfect. We ought to forever shake the Nineteenth Century camp meeting tirades that held moral perfection up as being synonymous with the Christian life. I can accept Wesley's idea of striving for perfection if perfection means purity of intention. I can't accept the perversion of his theology that assumed one had to be morally incorrupt before he could call himself a Christian. Yes, the New Testament says, "Be you therefore perfect." But that's an objective of the Christian faith, not a condition for membership in it.

To be a Christian — even a preacher — isn't dependent upon having arrived. It is to be en route. The Christian life is not where we are, but how we face. It's really whom we face. Conversion is not going from one place to another. It is turning around where we are. God does not call us to successfulness. God calls us to faithfulness.

Jesus did not ask his disciples to keep up with him. He asked them to follow after him. And they followed. They faltered, they failed. But they followed. They fumbled, they fell. But they followed.

I will follow. I will try to be honest, yet I will be dishonest at times. I will want to be real, but will be phony at points. I will desire to set a good example, yet I will lead some people astray. But I will follow. I can't be preacher if it means being perfect. I'll be me — warts and all — and I'll know, even when I mess it up, that it's not over for me. I'll know my father is the God who had in his company others who were vacillating and vulnerable, weak, and wayward.

Judas betrayed. Peter denied. Thomas doubted. Ananias and Sapphira cheated. Demas quit. John Mark ran home to mother. The Corinthians were stingy. The Galatians allowed themselves to be taken for suckers by false teachers.

I'll do all this and more. I'll flub the dub. I'll mess up a free lunch. But, in and through it all, I will know God never leaves nor forsakes me. I am loved. I am accepted. I am forgiven. Thank you, Lord.

CHAPTER 5

Sailing from a harbor

The prosecuting attorney snapped at me, "Your people are threatening my witness."

"What are you talking about?"

"These black people you brought up here."

"*I* brought? I'm not responsible for every black person in this county."

"You get out of this courthouse."

"It's my courthouse just as much as it is yours."

"You better leave or I'll have you thrown in jail. Get back in the pulpit where you belong."

Jail! Had I committed a crime? What I had done was to wade into the frigid water of social activism in a county where many think the church should keep hands off. Politicians are unaccustomed to a theology of involvement, and most church members are trapped in the stained-glass syndrome. The church is a country club (without a golf course) where nominal Christians exchange pleasantries and let the rest of the world go to hell.

The county I live in is the bedroom of Atlanta. Here people sleep, play bridge, and manicure their lawns. They also attend churches locked in by a dogmatic defense of the status quo.

"Come weal or come woe,
Our status is quo."

I have lived in two communities of my county, one white and one black. The contrast has been overwhelming. I knew that God condemns such inequities and I began to say so. I knew the church dares not constitute a reluctant caboose to the train of God's Kingdom on earth. I decided to stand for better. I knew that the gospel I was called to preach has a sword to show, and I began to wield it.

"What do you want?" the jailer asked.
"I would like to see Robert Jones."
"Ain't visiting hours."
"I'm a minister."
"You don't look like one."
"Here's my card."
"Oh, awright, he's in colored east."

I was escorted between two burly and bully guards. I was made to speak to Robert through mesh-covered bars. I was allowed two minutes and then ushered back past the jailer.

"What did you see that nigger for?"
"I'm Robert's pastor."
"God, Almighty! What's this world coming to?"

What, indeed, is this world coming to?

In the past, I had played the prophet, exhorting people to stop and consider this question. My stance had been a negative one and I had become an expert at picking the world apart, fault by fault. I'd warned, "Look what the world has come to."

Now I recognized that it isn't enough to be a caustic cynic; there is more. I had offered doom and no hope; judgment and no grace. I had said only, "Look what the world has come to." Now I began to tell and live the other side, "Look what has come to the world."

And listen to what He has come to do:

"I have come to preach the gospel to the poor.

"I have come to bring deliverance to the captives.

"I have come to set at liberty those who are oppressed." (Luke 4:18-19)

My jailer friend would say that's not new. It's not new, but it is fresh and current. That gospel message offends no one when it's nice little stories about what God *used* to do, but it offends like hell when applied to a segregated jail where Robert had been beaten and refused his medicine during an asthma attack. When I applied the gospel to that concrete situation, I had quit preachin' and gone to meddlin'.

The pulpit is not a wooden desk reserved for pious platitudes. It is the ground on which you stand when you confront a man with the basic issues of life. If the basic issues of life happen to be social change and political renewal, so be it.

She sat and sobbed, "I just don't understand it. He killed my husband. Why would they let him go?"

I turned and phoned the district attorney.

"Why did the jury acquit him?"

"I don't know."

"I thought it was an airtight case."

"All I know to tell you, Reverend, is that it was a typical all-white, all-male jury. As far as they were concerned, it was just one nigger killing another nigger. It didn't make any difference."

But it does make a difference! And the church ought to say so! The pulpit is a prophetic voice or else it deserves to be ignored and boycotted. The gospel is revolutionary by its very nature but we have turned it into sweetness and saccharin. We have no message, only a massage. We have no sword to cut, only a spoon to feed compromise and quiet consensus.

The church is not a museum for the display of mummy-wrapped saints. It is a harbor from which we sail to make a difference in our brother's life. As Saul Kane says in Masefield's poem,

I knew Christ had given me birth
to brother all the souls on earth.

I cannot be a brother and sit on my rear waiting for God to wave some magic wand and make it all better. I cannot be a Christian and ignore the crap and crud of injustice and inequity. I cannot be a theologian and confine my theology of the church to singing, preaching, and taking up a collection.

No, the church is a harbor from which we sail. I discovered this late; if I had discovered it earlier, I could have avoided the frustration and futility of playing church.

Now that I have heard the real gospel, the best days of my ministry are just ahead and the second best just behind. I've quit playing church. I've quit celebrating property rights. I've jumped off the ecclesiastical escalator.

I will not be part of a church that could repeat the history of Germany. That could happen, you know. Hitler hoped the German church would not hear the real gospel. He once told Pastor Niemoller, "You can deal with heaven. The German people on earth belong to me." The German Church stopped starkly still outside the narrow gate of obedience, and the German people fell before the onslaught of madness.

God, don't let that happen again! The trumpet to march into the reality of suffering has sounded. The clarion call to the real and raw of humanity's hurt is sounding. He who has ears, let him hear!

Will the church hear her marching orders, or will she continue to be a factory for conservative hypocrites? Will the church be captured by a basin-and-towel theology, or will she be controlled by sanctimonious snobs, ingrown and withdrawn? Jess Moody, in *A Drink at Joel's Place*, says the church has become about as self-contained as a house trailer, but there the comparison ends because house trailers are designed to *go somewhere*.

I know the church can go somewhere. I know the church can move and make a difference in the mass and mess of misery. I see some local congregations who are willing to die in order to live. I see ministers who are living a free style that is reminiscent of Jesus and who are willingly paying the price for it. I know laymen who have turned their communities around; through them, God has worked miracle after miracle.

I met with my administrative board and nearly choked as I spoke.

"I want you to know that the Children's Home of our conference is segregated."

"You mean they're asking us to give money to an institution that our children couldn't enter?"

"That's right."

"What should we do, Phil?"

"I think we should withhold our funds."

I expected their eager agreement, but they would have none of that. To a man, they vetoed my suggestion.

"We'd be doing the same thing that people have done to us," they said.

"You're right," I said, warming at their display of real Christianity.

"What's your plan?" I asked.

"We'll organize our support, then lobby and get the conference to change their policy."

Within six months it happened. Many other laymen and clergymen joined the battle as the church set her feet on higher ground. They knew Christ was ahead, punching holes in the darkness, and they went to meet him.

Now, the home has several black children, an interracial staff, and an interracial board of trustees. East Lake Church has continued to give its money and in increasing amounts. Two families serve as sponsor parents and seven of the white girls from the home play on our formerly all-black basketball team.

I'm glad our church didn't swallow my prescribed pill, which was full of despair mixed with revenge. Rather than withdraw in innocuous protest, our people decided to stay in the system and change it. They believed they had the moral power to change a hundred-year-old tradition. They did not see their church as a fortress in which to hide. They saw her as a harbor from which to sail. How proud I am of them!

Clergymen sell laymen short so many times! With some sort of a preacher paranoia, we assume the average church member can't wait to sabotage everything that is relevant, progressive, and future-oriented. That's not true! Laymen often don't do any more because clergymen don't ask any more. The church will move like a mighty army when ministers, both lay and clergy, are captured by the gospel hope and clothed in the gospel power. Our aim is too low!

"They sell rotten meat, pay low wages, and every store they have stinks."

"What can we do about it?"

"We'll bargain with them."

"What if they won't negotiate?"

"We'll boycott until they do."

The boycott was called. One store was assigned to me. I had never done anything like this before. I turned to my congregation.

"I want you to help me bring this off."

"When do you want us to walk?"

I went to our members with my clipboard in hand. A white suburbanite responded, "Put somebody black with me. I'll feel safer."

A thirteen-year-old reluctantly volunteered, "I'll do it but don't tell grandmother."

A brawny factory hand answered, "I'll be there right after the first shift."

For days, we marched and carried aloft our signs. Every time I was about to quit, one of our members would say, "Keep on, I'll be there to help you as soon as I hop off the bus."

The day came when the phone rang and we were summoned to the table to negotiate. We received every consideration we wanted. I was happy for the employees and customers. I was glad that justice had triumphed. I was overjoyed that I was a part of a church that knew what servanthood and meaningful martyrdom were all about.

Many have come to give their all just when the bottom was about to fall out.

He was nearly 70 years old when he came to see me.

"I've noticed circles under your eyes," he said.

"It's rough just trying to keep the doors open."

"I want to help you."

"I really need your help."

"If you want, I'll be your full-time administrative assistant. I'll expect no pay."

"Then you're part of the team!"

"Write me a job description. I'll pick it up next week."

That was four years ago. Since then, C. B. Farrar has been the greatest testimony to a sense of Christian vocation of anyone I know, and the best administrative assistant this side of everywhere.

There are many others who have wanted their church to be a harbor from which to sail. There is the couple who stayed when most of their friends and family left. They do whatever is necessary to get the job done. His cool business head has gotten us through many a financial dilemma. In those early days, she held the church ladies together when it looked like the bottom would fall out; she also taught a girl's sewing class every week for four years.

There is another family who watched from a distance for a while and then drew closer. He once said, "I don't know if I'll ever change from Baptist to Methodist, but if I do, I'll be the best member you have." He was telling the truth. He now heads up an athletic program at East Lake Church that involves nearly 100 young people, and his wife is one of our best teachers. He is also handyman deluxe, and a frequently heard phrase around the church is: "We better call Willie."

These are a few examples of the men and women who have taken seriously God's call to wash feet and deliver captives. They have helped me to see the vision of the church when once I saw only her perversion. The church ain't down yet because there are countless ministers, both lay and clergy, who know where it's at in terms of need — who know where to get it in terms of power.

Even the gates of hell will not prevail against a church like that!

I had been at East Lake Church not quite a year when Martin Luther King, Jr., was assassinated. A skinny, white doctoral candidate came by and said, "We should open this church up for the funeral."

"What do you mean?"

"We'll bring in beds and food and take care of visitors from out of town."

"Who will do it?"

"Your congregation, Phil. Your congregation."

They did it. They met people at the airport and brought them to the church building. They met people at the bus station and took them to Ebenezer Baptist Church to view the body. People were housed and fed.

One white member called to complain. "I don't know what all the fuss is about. It's just someone else who has died."

When I hung up, I was shaken. But just then another white member, a cab driver, called.

"I haven't been to church for a long time but I'm coming next Sunday."

"Why the change?"

"You know you sent me to the airport?"

"Yes."

"Well, I just chauffeured Leslie Uggams all over town. That's quite a church you have!"

Two ladies had worked all day following the funeral folding blankets and sweeping floors. As they were leaving the church, I said, "Thank you for helping."

"We had no choice."

"I'm proud of the way people responded, aren't you?"

"Yes, I think something has started here this weekend that will never stop."

It never will. People from all walks and ways of life have come together to be The Body of Christ. For them, the church is much more than property, architecture, budget. The church is a harbor from which they sail.

CHAPTER 6

Resting in a haven

To set sail is not enough. To march as a social activist — and nothing else — is foolish. You will bleed to death on the jagged rocks of the chasms you seek to bridge.

The church is a harbor from which we sail, true. But the church is also a haven in which we rest. The outward journey demands an inward journey. The secularist must be a pietist, too.

I was ten years old when my Sunday School teacher said, "Prayer is the most important thing for you to learn."

"But there's more to being a Christian than praying," I challenged.

"Yes, but remember what Jesus said: 'This kind goes forth but by prayer and fasting.' "

When I was in seminary in the early Sixties and reflected on this teacher's arguments, I didn't think he knew what he was talking about. Now there is no argument. Then, I thought relevance was having a pas-

sion for picketing. Now, although I frequently find
myself on the picket line, I know there is much more.

I walked in a steady drizzle
of rain when he came out the door
He jabbed me in the ribs with his
elbow and muttered, "damn troublemaker."
I wanted to hit him. I would have
but I remembered, "love your enemies."
I kept on walking.
He watched a minute and went on down the
street. I prayed. "Thank you for strength."

There is a strength which a social activist must have
or he will fizzle out. So many have. The soapbox liberals
soon run out of soap and fade away. There has to be
another dimension.

Most of the militants that I know about don't have
this extra edge. They have the passion and the courage,
but they lack the spiritual resources for the long haul.
Their zeal goes untempered by wisdom and their enthusiasm has no sustaining power. What good is an
Eldridge Cleaver in exile, or a Huey Newton in jail?

Most of the radicals within the church don't have it
either. They lack what the Quakers call "peace at the
center." They run off half-cocked, fighting their potential allies and defeating their own purposes. They end
up with no position of influence to use and no people
to lead. Some wind up on a national board traveling the
world as an expert-in-residence, influencing few and
robbing God of a servant who could have made a difference. Others end up in a specialty, tucked away in
some remote corner and ignored. The countryside is

crowded with dropouts and copouts. They had the right idea — they were committed to love, justice, and power. But they ran out of gas!

Before we can be successful in the streets, we must first be saturated in the sanctuary. We must be immersed in the experience of worship through praise and adoration. We must be baptized in the experience of prayer and seeking. We must be honest students of *the Word* before a word of relevance will come from our lips. There will be no successful social struggle until there is serious spiritual strength.

We were at a New Year's Eve party when he said, "I can't figure you out."

"What do you mean?"

"I've been listening to what you say, and you sound like a fundamentalist. But I know what you do, and the two don't fit."

But they *do* fit! If the church gives her people nothing but a cause and a protest, they will starve to death on the very streets that they seek to cleanse through their social action.

We are on a course which threatens to repeat the mistake of the social gospel of 19th Century Liberalism, which, as Marney points out, assumed that "God and The Kingdom were values at which you arrived and not sources from which you started." If they could just get everybody fed and clothed and cured of alcoholism, the Kingdom would come.

Not so, and this was the downfall of the social gospel.

The branches of service will bear no fruit unless they spring from the roots of a personal encounter with Almighty God.

Nineteenth Century Liberalism set 18th Century Pietism on its ear — and well it should have, for 18th Century Pietism didn't have it, either. It did not see man's response to God's love on either a corporate or a social scale. It began and ended with individual conversion. That's not good enough.

However, 19th Century Liberalism threw the baby out with the bath water. It became so rational and scientific that it stripped God of His humanity. It took away His personhood. Nineteenth Century Liberalism had no real doctrine of the Father and soon shot its wad.

The social gospel was not enough in the 19th Century and any resurrection of it under a new name in the 20th Century won't be enough, either. We must be involved, but first we must be empowered. We must feed our brothers, but first we must be fed ourselves. We need a body, but we must have a soul, also.

There is a story about a sculptor who was so skilled he could make anything. One day he decided to make a man. He assembled his material and began to work. He made a body, and what a body it was! On that body he placed a masterful head.

When he was almost finished, his creation spoke to him:

"Master, give me a soul."

It so frightened the sculptor that he ran from the studio with his creation close behind, pleading, "Master, give me a soul; you have made me a magnificent body. Now give me a soul!"

We must have the body of political and social action. We also need a soul. Listen to a poignant statement from the pen of Dag Hammarskjold: "The more faithfully you listen to the voice within you, the better you will hear what is sounding outside."

We must see it like it is. We must tell it like it is. But first, we must know who we are. We are children of God, made in His image — an image fed by honest prayer, prudent study, and personal commitment. We need a haven in which to rest. We need a soul.

There are many things about the church of my childhood and youth which I now stand against. It is ironic that the spiritual strength that enables me to criticize an exclusive, ingrown, comatose institution came from just such an institution. God works through us before He's finished in us. That's as true of the church as it is of individuals and is one reason I'm still in the fold.

He worked through Calvary Church in Moundsville, West Virginia, and her spiritual giants.

She pressed me. "Go on and pray out loud."

I said, "But I can't."

"How are you going to be a preacher if you can't pray?"

"I don't want to be a preacher."

"Well, you ought to know how to pray anyway."

We were drummed and drilled. Bible verses were taught by rote and young people were persistently challenged to pray in public. We were made to memorize long speeches for special assemblies. I can remember reading the scripture lesson when I had to be put on a stool to reach the pulpit.

This method of Christian education has been severely criticized, and it should be if it does not come out our fingertips in deeds of love for our brother. Right now, I wouldn't trade the drumming and drilling for any book by Tillich I've ever read. It has been my armor in many a tight squeeze — for example, when the officer rang our doorbell.

"This is for you."

"What is it, sir?"

"It's a summons. You're being sued for the boycott."

"I am?"

"Yes, take this please."

I took the paper and moved slowly away from the door. I didn't know Lisa had been watching.

She asked, "Daddy, are they going to take you to jail?"

"No, I don't think so."

"I love you, daddy."

"I love you too, honey."

I slumped on the bed. I was exhausted and confused. Those words which had been spoken to me as a ten-year-old came back:

"Remember what Jesus said: 'This kind goes forth but by prayer and fasting.' "

Jesus was right and he's been right every time I've been between a rock and a hard place — damned if I do and damned if I don't.

"You must leave the dance."

"We ain't gonna'."

"I will not have you in here drunk and with those knives."

"You'll have to make us."

I prayed, "O God, be with me," and then said to them, "I can if you force me."

I took a step. They smiled and left.

The Bible verses I learned by rote have come back again and again to glue me together when I was about to fall apart. The exercises in prayer have given me a well of living water from which I drink every day. The steady, rock-like faith of the sung and unsung heroes of God's Kingdom has put underneath me everlasting arms. I thank God for a church that is a harbor in which to rest.

When I went to seminary, I suppressed my early religious training. I didn't want anyone to call me a "fundy." Besides, the people back in my home church had no outreach, and I had become their most severe critic. Their Christian life style was incomplete. My trouble was that I had gone overboard in my campaign for reform.

"We meet at 7:30 each morning in the chapel."

"I don't have time."

"You don't have time to *pray*?"

"I have more important things to do."

I resisted every professor who was the least bit pious. Some of them deserved it, for they were intolerant and narrow. Others were honest and open and I missed the contents because I didn't like the wrapper.

The pendulum began a swing in the other direction when I spent two post-seminary years as associate to a man who held the same basic social objectives that I held and, at the same time, believed in searching the scriptures and kneeling in prayer.

The nudge was gentle but became more forceful when, two years later, I found myself a circuit rider out in the middle of nowhere. I resented having been sent there, and just knew I'd die on the vine. There weren't many people — just a lot of chickens and cows and loneliness.

As we chatted at my mail box, Jim Coad said,

"Would you mind praying with a couple of Presbyterians?"

"What makes you think I need it?"

"It's obvious."

Out of futility and frustration, I met once a week with the two fellow pastors. They didn't *talk* about prayer, they *prayed!* I was cynical and caustic, yet I knew they had something I wanted and needed. They faced the same desert, but they had a song to sing. My lips were mute.

I began to cry out, "Lord, teach me to pray! There must be other resources. The well I drink from is dry."

Blinders fell and vistas which heretofore I had put down as fanatical and superstitious opened before my eyes. Faintheartedness and loneliness were replaced by power, perseverance, and presence.

I bolted through the door.

"Margaret Anne! Come here!"

"Something's happened to you."

"How do you know?"

"There's joy in your face."

Something — rather, *somebody* — had happened to me. For the first time in my life, I was undeniably convinced of the Holy Spirit working in me. I was intoxicated!

The situations I had deemed impossible remained, but there was zest and zeal, faith and fortitude. I prayed a prayer and felt a power.

I now would be able to do something about the social impulses that were so strong in my mind and heart. I had been able to talk the talk; now I could walk the walk. And so when the chance came to plant my feet in the middle of a social revolution at East Lake, I was ready to go. And I didn't go alone.

The need for the church to have a secularist-pietist blend is one of my firmest convictions. We waste so much time and talent arguing over *which* of the two when we could have the *best* of *both* worlds. There are ministers sent to progressive suburban churches who spend all their energy trying to eliminate social activism and replace it with spiritual renewal. There are laymen who spend all their energy trying to teach those young turks a little good old-time religion.

Denominational bodies are split into camps, and as the categories harden, fellowship deteriorates. Clergymen who need each other so much never get close enough to lean on their brother because he's one of those "spirit-filled boys." Clergymen, who need the laymen's witness of faith, won't get near because that faith is too simple and is anti-intellectual. Laymen who have left the church because it doesn't have enough social relevance need to get back in — the church has less because they left, and it needs more, not less. These laymen must challenge a system that ignores humanity's hurt and be ready to receive the witness of spiritual renewal others have to give. Other laymen must use the prayer life, which they cherish so much, to ask God to keep them open to the cutting edge of revolution.

The case for the secularist-pietist blend has been made in many places by accomplished and articulate scholars. It has never been stated better than in the ninth chapter of Mark.

It was a summit meeting of the top four powers — Jesus, Peter, James, and John. There was challenging conversation, powerful praying, and wild ecstasy.

They were so stimulated that they bargained for an extension. "Lord, this is a pleasant relief from the choking dust of the open road. Being up here (in this rarefied air) is almost like being in heaven. Down there — well, Lord, don't get us wrong, but those people are starting to bug us with all their aches and complaints. Can't we stay up here just a little bit longer?"

At the bottom of the mountain, the remaining nine had set about to relate with relevance. They were relieved that they didn't have to go on the mountaintop retreat. "It seems all Jesus wants to do lately is to pray," they said. "There are too many important things to be done to spend so much time on your knees. This is where it's at, down here at the grass roots."

The men on the mountain were right, but only half-right. The servants in the streets were right, but only half-right.

Jesus constrained the inner circle to descend to where people were hurting; he reprimanded them for dodging the issues. Jesus also challenged those below to take their spiritual condition more seriously; he reminded them there would be no healing without prayer and fasting.

Jesus knew the power-filled amalgamation of quietism and activism. Jesus always stood with one foot on the mountain and one foot in the valley. Jesus was both pietist and secularist. We miss the message when we think in terms of *either-or*.

As I face the future of the church, I know she must be able to hold this blend if she is to have purpose and power. The church must walk simultaneously on the mountains of transfiguration and in the valley of the demon-possessed. She must be both spiritual and social; both reverent and relevant. She must be on two journeys at the same time — one inward and one outward. The people of Christ cannot begin before they pray. Neither can they stop after they pray.

The church, as the instrument for implementing who we are and what we are about, must provide us a fellowship with which we can walk both the mountains of spiritual exuberance and the valleys of humanizing involvement. The church must be a haven in which we rest and a harbor from which we sail.

CHAPTER 7

Stepladder syndrome

I hadn't seen him since seminary days and we had a lot of catching up to do.

"How many members do you have?"

"About 325."

"What's your budget?"

"A little over $50,000."

"Gee, when you were in seminary, we thought you would go right to the top."

So did I. I had it all plotted out. As a novice pastor, I would have no choice but to spend two years in the sticks. But I planned to hit the ground running. Within a few months, I would have the whole county in love with me. I would reform, renew, and revolutionize that little parish until it became a showplace for Methodism. The Candler School of Theology would point to it as a demonstration of great pastoral leadership. Soon, the county-seat church would beg me to come and do the same for them. I would stay there four years and move on to the big city. I would be the star of suburbia with the fastest-growing congregation in the history of the conference. From suburbia to downtown. From downtown to a district superintendency — to the episcopacy — to the right hand of God!

Move over James and John. I want both the right hand and the left hand. Here *I* come. Move over Peter. I want the keys to the Kingdom. Here *I* come! Make another spot in the Trinity. Here *I* come!

The chart was drawn and the course was set. The ecclesiastical escalator was going up and I was on it. The heavens were open and the rising young star on the horizon was me. I was struttin' in the name of the Lord!

I was suffering from the stepladder syndrome but didn't know it. I said I wanted to serve in Christ's name, but what I really wanted was to move one rung higher on my way to superstar status. The goal was the top. The plan was to work hard, be Mr. Personality, and play my cards right.

I soon learned that one guarantee to success is to build great physical monuments to the glory of God. The lesson came early in seminary.

"Boys," the professor lectured, "if you are going to make it to the top, remember this: You must build something everywhere you go."

I believed him and arose to testify:

"When I was in college, I served a three-point circuit in Appalachia. At Spurlock, I built a two-hole outhouse. Does that count?"

The class laughed. True, I was only half-serious. But I was dead serious about assuring myself a place in the heavens of ecclesiastical distinction. If it took building programs, I'd already had a very successful one. I'd provided a place for man's basic need.

Now, I know better. I know the monuments to God are usually monuments to some preacher's ego. The countryside is covered with overbuilt and overadorned temples which were constructed so Second Church Harry could get to First Church.

The Peter Principle describes structurophilia as "an obsessive concern with buildings — their planning, construction, maintenance, and reconstruction — and an increasing unconcern with the work that is going on, is supposed to be going on, inside them." Many ministers are structurophiliacs.

I grabbed another handle to pull me to the top. It's called ministerial etiquette. It's really saying the right thing to the right people at the right time. It's dressing like a preacher, talking like a preacher, and acting like a preacher.

I dashed to the discount house to buy an austere black suit to go with my sedate black shoes. I practiced in the empty sanctuary until my stained glass voice was reminiscent of the great preachers of yesteryear. I watched carefully what I said lest it be unbecoming of a man of the cloth. I suppressed my anger. I denied my humor.

I castrated myself. In order to get to the top, I became a third sex (men, women, and preachers). I had forgotten that in heaven there are saints, in hell there are sinners, and in the church there are both. The sinner's list includes Charlie Cleric, too.

Every aspiring actor or athlete has a hero whom he

seeks to emulate. I picked me out several preachers who were on the top rung and I imitated them. They were pious and pompous. For a time, I tried to be a Holy Joe.

I saw another prerequisite for certain advance. A minister must be an authority on a variety of subjects. His dossier should be entitled, "Anything You Always Wanted To Know About Everything and Have Only Now Learned Where To Ask." People come to us for help and we advise when we should listen. We push a button and out rolls a prescription. We feel obligated to have a fast, fancy formula and a right, ready remedy. After all, how can we get to the heights of the system if we don't know our stuff?

To rise to the top, one should be informed and informing. More important than what you know, however, is who you know (or nose). You can dress the part and talk the part and still flounder in a mess of mediocrity. You must push, yes, but the *pull* is more significant.

I learned this when I first went to seminary. I was from out of state and had no connections. I was also out of money. I desperately needed a job.

"I hear you have a youth director's job."

"Yes, who recommended you?"

"No one. I saw it on the theology school bulletin board."

"Well, I've sort of promised it to another young man. The bishop from Alabama called about him last night."

I said thank you and hung up. I tried another church. I kept trying for over a year. I couldn't get a job because I didn't know anybody.

There are hundreds of bright and able men in our

conference systems all over the country who are hopelessly unchallenged and unrewarded because they don't know anybody. They can't even make it *to* the stepladder because they're trapped on the treadmill. They are bounced from one nothing charge to another nothing charge because there's no district superintendent who will elbow for them. They may have a district superintendent who is, himself, so much a prisoner of the system that he won't open his mouth lest his patrons shoot him down.

Some of these capable men keep plugging away, hoping for a break. They serve well and go to their graves never having been given a challenge that matched their potential. Others become bitter, lose incentive, perform ineffectively, and waste away in a never-ending whirlwind of almost-opportunities.

Of course, there are parallels in all occupations and professions. When I worked in an Ohio Valley steel mill, I saw men become foremen because they were related to somebody in management. In a Georgia textile company, even the senior vice-president is vulnerable to a coup if someone can put together more influence than he possesses. In a public utility company, longtime employees are kept down at the whim of an insecure and threatened supervisor. City politicians get better committee appointments if they play golf with the mayor.

If at first you don't succeed, try, try again to find a sponsor who will pull you up by the bootstrap. Sometimes your senior minister will give you a boost unless he's afraid you might get *his* job. Don't look to your contemporaries to help you unless they're already four steps up the ladder ahead of you. Maybe the district superintendent will mention you in the right places. Just remember how to spell his name when the next election comes around.

We have forgotten whom to worship. Our creeds are all wrong.

I believe in:

God the Father, Son, and Bishop —
God the Father, Son, and building program —
God the Father, Son, and First Church —
and a $50,000 parsonage — and approval of all
     the laymen—
appointment to a big board — election to general
     conference — and on and on.

Integrity will not come until we crash our idols, O Men of Athens, and worship the true God. There will be no deed of social relevance until we act because God speaks. There will be no recovery of the church until we have an audacity born of freedom from the pressure of getting to the next rung.

After ten years of suffering from the stepladder syndrome, I know now what is important is not Second Church or even First Church — not lay consensus or clergy approval — but the Word of God. I finally became aware that I was following the church and not the Lord. I wanted to be a fat cat. Oh, the games preachers play!

The first time I jumped off the ladder was eight months after I became pastor of East Lake Church. *The Atlanta Constitution* picked up an article I had written in our newsletter concerning the "breath-holding" open-door policy of many of Atlanta's churches. I had accused those churches of opening their doors, then holding their breath and hoping no one would come. I had indicted them for unfriendliness to blacks who were let in and for failing to include blacks in follow-up visitation. The Monday after my piece was reprinted, I was summoned by the big bear of bureaucracy to holy headquarters. I was reminded of the conference subsidy on our building indebtedness.

"Young man, don't bite the hand that feeds you."

I shook a little when I realized that I might be about to cut my own throat. I was quickly picked up by Presence, and I heard myself say:

"I understood that when we received this money, there would be no strings attached. If I have to compromise convictions to have conference support, you better get somebody else. I will not lower my voice to raise the budget."

Go on. Jump off the ecclesiastical escalator. But, now hear this! *You might get hurt!* You do bite the hand that feeds you!

I challenged a big-name for his patronizing attitude toward the blacks in our conference.

He stood on his tiptoes and shouted, "I don't know who you think you are, telling us what to do. You're not dry behind the ears in the conference. I guess we ought to elect you pope and let you pontificate to all of us!"

I muttered a half-hearted "everyone to his own opinion" and walked away, feeling sick in my gut. I recognized that when it came time for me to move, this man would have much to say about where I would live and where my children would go to school. He could affect my salary. I had that uncertain feeling that plagues so many who are pawns of an itinerant bureaucracy. (I'm sure that school teachers, postal clerks, and branch bank managers know what I mean). After my venture, I longed for the security of the stepladder. I wanted back on the escalator.

To resist the bureaucracy is more dangerous than to break up a fight between knife-wielding maniacs. To be your own man in the ministry is to invite pain far more serious than the pain that comes from any crank phone call.

As I began to challenge the traditions of the system, I did so with emotions of faith mixed with fear, courage with cowardice, readiness with reluctance. Thank God for the strength and power that returned again and again to wipe away my tears and set my feet back in the path. Thank God that His Holy Spirit is not an attic antique covered with the dust of bygone years. Thank God for the peace and power of Presence. Thank God there is a haven as well as a harbor.

There is a great irony in all of this. Once I jumped off the ecclesiastical escalator, thereby curing myself of stepladder syndrome, I felt free to stay in the institutional church. This freedom came after I asked God to release me from the commitment made by an 18-year-old boy crying at the altar and promising "I'll be your preacher the rest of my life." God did release me, and a new commitment took shape. It was a commitment of honest vulnerability. It was one with the open options of other occupations. It was a commitment that shook me loose from my false identity images of ecclesiastical grandeur.

When I broke the syndrome, I went through an identity crisis akin to the one I experienced when I moved into the black community.

Who am I outside of the system? Who will tell me who I am when the system is no longer interested? Who will I be when I am divested of the security of going up the ladder? Can I give up my dream of superstar status? What will I do if I leave the clergy? What *can* I do? Where else can I go to work out my theology of servanthood? What other group or institution can satisfy my need for community?

These are rough questions to struggle with, but I'm glad I didn't run from them. In the struggle, I have discovered who the Lord and Master of my life really is. I don't need the institution to tell me who I am. I know who I am.

I'm a child of God and a servant of Christ. I'm a slave to Jesus and I'm free of sucking at the tit of ecclesiastical preferment. I'm free to stay in the church, following what light God gives me. I'm able to seek and speak His Word — even if the walls of the tabernacle fall down upon me.

I think I'm able, but sometimes I wonder. One day, I went to see the bishop about our conference's strategy for transitional churches. I decided to check on another matter while I was there.

"Bishop, there's one more thing I want to mention before I leave."

"I want to hear about it."

"I'm not ready to leave East Lake, but we both know I can't stay there forever."

"Yes, you'll need to move on someday."

"When I do, what kind of situation do you foresee for me?"

"Well, I hadn't really thought about it. We have an itinerant system and you're an itinerant minister. When the time comes, we'll find a place for you."

I wanted to scream, "That's what's wrong with our system — *a preacher for a place; a place for a preacher.*" I wanted to protest, "I'm a *person*, with feelings and a family — not a rotating commodity!"

I said nothing of the kind. I merely said, "Thank you, sir" and left. (I might as well have said, "Yas suh, Boss," and then shuffled on home.)

God, make me so free I can live it and not just write about it in a book. Amen.

CHAPTER 8

Sorry, I'm playin' with the kids

We were all on the floor playing our girls' favorite game. Each player has a plastic tree with ten cherries on it and a little white bucket. You flip the spinner and then take off or put on the number of cherries that the spinner directs. The first player to get all his cherries off the tree and into the bucket wins the game.

Kara was about to win her first game *ever* when the phone rang. I went to the phone hoping for a wrong number.

"Hello."

"Is this the preacher?"

"This is Phil Barnhart."

"I have to see you right away."

"What does it concern?"

"It's about our attempts to get more police protection."

"I want to hear about it, but I'm tied up right now."

"When can I see you?"

"First thing in the morning."

"I don't know if I can wait."

"I'm afraid you'll have to. Tonight, I'm playin' with the kids."

I never thought I'd be that direct. I had committed myself to climbing the ladder, and you don't advance by alienating your congregation. If you want to get to the top, you have to placate the people. That means holding Aunt Suzy's hand when she has the flu. It means running on Monday to see Mr. Smith because on Sunday he had that "you haven't been to visit me lately" look on his face. It means continuous and tedious luncheons with the chairman of the board, for he's the man who can make you or break you.

There was an old layman, devout,
  Who packed a mosaical clout.
In faith and in morals,
  He won all his quarrels.
He's in and the parson is out.
                    —Chad Walsh

No man wants to be out. The young junior executive has his eyes on the senior vice-president's suite, plush and prestigious. In his drive to get that suite, he puts in a 65-hour work week. He drops by on Saturday to tidy up his desk, hoping that at least one superior will see him there. He attends cocktail parties that he doesn't enjoy. He takes his work home at night. His den is a replica of his office, complete with telephone, dicta-phone, calculator, the works.

I know many men who aren't executives and have this

same obsession. They work both a regular job and a part-time job. They slave all day on a General Motors assembly line and then do "a little janitorial work" at night. Some of my friends work two eight-hour shifts every day of the year. A few do it because it's necessary if they're to feed a wife and eight kids. They are not skilled enough or educated enough or white enough to get a good day's pay for a hard day's work so they work two jobs to make one salary. Many, however, work extra out of a thirst for success and status. They'll never be bank president — but there are other standards of success. They can have a bigger house in a new community. Their Ford can give way to a Cadillac. For the very industrious, their children might escape from ghetto education to a nice private school. There is a top rung for every man — and there is a way of getting to the top. The price is steep, but there is a way.

A minister is no exception. He's a man with drives and ambitions. He, too, has his eyes on the pinnacle. He, too, will pay the price.

I paid the price for a long time. But I knew I'd gone too far when, one day, Margaret Anne announced:

"Amy walked today."

"That's great! At 13 months. Lisa was 15 months, wasn't she?"

"Yes — and Kara was 14 months."

"I don't remember that . . . Amy will be talking soon. Lisa was 20 months when she talked, wasn't she?"

"That's right — and Kara was 19 months."

"I don't remember that . . ."

Kara was five months old when I moved to East Lake Church. I arrived with a dedication to make that situation blossom even if I had to work 24 hours a day. I maintained a vigorous visitation schedule, and there was something going on at the church day and night. The congregation was growing. So was Kara, and I was missing it!

It was shortly after this realization that I stood before the congregation and made a little speech I should have made earlier.

"You are my people. I love each of you very much. I want to be a real pastor to you. I also have a family that is very special to me. I must and I will spend an appropriate amount of time with them. I'm not their pastor, but I am their husband and father. To be a good husband and father takes a lot of time and energy. I plan to give that to my loved ones.

"You know me well enough by now to believe I'm serious. I know you well enough to believe you understand and agree.

"Sometimes you may call me to ask me to pray or to speak at a special meeting and I'll tell you I have a previous engagement. That engagement might well be a night at the drive-in movie with my wife and children. You might need to talk to me and I'll tell you I have an appointment. My appointment might be to stay at home and talk to my family.

"And, please, don't call me on Friday night. That's my night to howl! Margaret Anne and I court on Friday nights. We need our time together. Call only if you're dyin' and, then, think about it twice.

"All that I've said about my family applies to each family in this congregation. Spend a lot of time together. Share your interests. Express your love. We'll all be happier because of it."

God called me to be a minister, but first I was called to be a man. I am committed to the gospel mission, but I have four lovely ladies at my house whom I will not sacrifice at the altar of professional ambition. If I am to be a responsible man, I can't go furiously flitting after the dubious prize of congregational approval while leaving the children to become psychological orphans.

Many ministers are so married to the ambition of making all the folks love them that their sweet young bride is neglected, ignored, and turned off. The only reason the divorce rate among ministers doesn't soar is the fact that our wives are often as victimized by the stepladder syndrome as we are. We'd be men more than we've ever been before if our wives would flat out announce, "Either divorce yourself from that church or divorce yourself from me!" We'd scurry to get home on time and spend a few evenings with the family. If for no other reason, we'd do it because divorce is scandalous and you never get to the top that way.

Congregational approval and the ecclesiastical escalator are the same bag. If I'm to achieve the next rung in my dream world, the people must be impressed. Then, when the pastoral committee writes its annual letter, the district superintendent will also be impressed. When the district superintendent (who sits in the Cabinet) speaks in my behalf at appointment time, the bishop will be impressed. I'll be on my way to the next plateau.

I'll get my promotion. The rising star will be right on schedule. But I'll lose everything else. My family will be loyal out of duty and not out of love. The colleagues I've gathered will bolt the gate the first time I've slipped a rung. The sensitive and honest members of my congregation will know me for the phony I am.

We strain and strut so our people will tell us who they think we are. I wish you laymen would tell us what you really think. Don't give us that pious stuff — "He's a wonderful, dedicated Christian man." Tell it like it is. "He's playin' a game. He's full of crap!" Laymen, don't let us con you. We'll do it everytime!

When a minister sells out to the political expediency of scratching backs and kissing rear-ends, he loses the most powerful witness he has. When he is so busy mending fences and putting out fires that he has no time, energy, or even inclination to be a man at home, he is just a great big phony in the eyes of those who know where it's at. Phooey on a phony like that!

Don't you laymen listen to our tender sermons about recovering the family unless the proof is in the puddin'. Don't you politicians in the congregation pay any attention to our tirades against compromised convictions until we quit sacrificing our families for a First Church plum. Don't you listen to all that stuff about a family altar — not when we can't even kiss the kids good night because we're having a peace conference with our top money man.

One day, I had scheduled appointments back to back with a variety of people for a variety of reasons. Unbeknown to me, a close friend of mine from another part of the state had been waiting downstairs in the church office. When there was a break in my schedule, my secretary showed him in.

"Do you know what you remind me of?" he demanded.

"What?"

"An old bitch dog."

"A what?"

"An old bitch dog."

"I don't know what you mean."

"Have you ever seen an old bitch dog just after she had pups?"

"Yes, I have."

"You know how the little pups hang onto her tits for dear life?"

"Yes."

"Well, that's what you remind me of. An old bitch dog with the pups hangin' on."

He made his point. The people in and out of my office were the pups and I was the bitch dog. I was working in a frenzy just to keep everybody happy. I did what everybody wanted because I was going right to the top. Some of what went on was important, most of it was not. I never said no, for that very person might one day keep me from being king. I wanted to be king!

I don't want it anymore. At least, not enough to campaign for it. I guess I'd take the scepter if drafted, but that doesn't happen in any bureaucracy. The top rung is there, but the price is too high. I want to sleep at night. I want to be me, not some robot of an organization man programmed by selfish ambition. Carlyle

Marney says it better than I've heard from anyone else:

"Twenty-five or so years ago I set out to Holy City determined to be one of the new breed. On my blithe way I took three oaths: (1) I would never become economically victimized by a job. (2) I would never want anything a denomination could give me to the point of paying too much to get it. (3) I would follow new light into any place as soon as I knew it to be new light."

I will not pay the price of neglecting my wife, scarring my children, and disillusioning my real friends by becoming something I'm really not. I will not sink to the bottom in order to climb to the top.

I won't become what I myself will not recognize. I will not lose my identity. I am me!

I will not be victimized by corporateness. Squeeze me too tightly into a compartmentalized category and I will explode.

I will not be dictated by institutionalism. Insist that I swallow whatever comes from the big bear of bureaucracy and I will spit in your eye.

I will not be driven by tradition. Preach to me that I should do this or that because someone else has and I will mock the parade, for it is a fool's parade.

I will not sell my soul to secure my status. If you call me to speak to a group or to meet with a man in order that I can be seen in the right place at the right time with the right people — "Sorry, I'm playin' with the kids."

CHAPTER 9

And yet so far away

In this book, I've said a lot about being my own man and doing my own thing. I've vowed not to be trapped in the stepladder syndrome. I've promised not to sacrifice my family at the altar of congregational approval. I've refused to wear the preacher mask. I've said I will resist any classification by category.

That all sounds good. I can talk the talk with the best of them. Can I walk the walk? I'm long on pronouncement and short on performance. I have great starting power but little staying power.

Every man dreams of being free and yet is painfully aware of his chains. A coach wants to inspire his boys to live a free style, so he talks of integrity. But when his team loses, his hand is slapped by alumni and parents who want to win at any cost. He goes back to business as usual.

A poverty program director believes what his training taught him about delivering power to the people. He promotes a grass-rooter to a top spot in the organization.

The grass-rooter has experience (eight years of on-the-job training) and is a community resident, but he doesn't meet the guidelines from bureaucratic downtown. The director is told to shape up or ship out. He goes back to business as usual.

Every man wants to be free, but there is a point at which any of us can be bought off. There is a level of bribery at which everyone has his price. During the Civil War, a Union commodore was put in charge of a blockade on the Mississippi with strict orders to allow no cotton to pass down the river. Some businessmen tried to obtain release of their cotton by bribing the commodore. They visited him and promised a generous price if he would let two barges pass through. Without looking up from his desk, he refused. They raised the price and he answered with an emphatic "No!" They raised it again and the commodore jumped from his chair, seized one of them by the collar and threw him out the door. "Out with you!" he shouted to them. "You're getting too close to my price!"

I thought I was a free man. I had taken an oath not to let the system compromise my convictions. If I had to, I would bite the hand that fed me.

Then, I sat at a session of my annual conference listening to a report on the voting for general conference delegates. I was getting some votes and it looked like I might have a chance. I became excited over the prospect and quite puffed up about my popularity. It isn't often a man my age is elected to general conference, and for a moment I had visions of grandeur. It was a fleeting moment, for I didn't even make it to jurisdictional conference. Through my style of ministry, I had polarized the voters and so I couldn't get beyond my hard core of faithful supporters. People would rather fight than switch to me. Nevertheless, for several ballots I was in the running and was basking in the glory.

During this time, capital funds legislation came to the floor for approval. Included in the package was $100,000 for a communications project that nobody knew anything about. The whole conference sat there and let it go through untouched. There wasn't one challenging question. We never once said anything about priorities. We didn't know whether the money was to be spent for salaries, property, training, or what. We slept on.

Meanwhile, however, I scribbled a speech on the back of an envelope, then moved to the edge of my seat. I would be the conscience of the conference. I raised my hand to get the bishop's attention. When the bishop didn't see me right away, I lowered my hand. I slid back in the seat and put my speech in my pocket. Well, I had tried, hadn't I?

At other annual conferences, I had moved boldly to make my point. I had jumped to the floor to get in my two cents' worth. I had spoken freely and honestly. But now I sat mute.

I was irritated at myself for having held my peace. I was nauseated, because I knew why I had slid back: I didn't want to lose any votes! I feared I would alienate my supporters. I was afraid I would discourage those who might turn to me when their candidate faded.

I was right back on the stepladder. I had fancied myself free, but I could still be bought. The price was a

little higher, but I was still for sale. In pursuit of freedom, I had come close; yet freedom was so far away! In
making my choice, I had failed to choose my integrity.

Of *integrity*, David O. Woodyard says:

"The root meaning of the word suggests that it is a
state of being undivided; it is that quality of being which
on crucial issues cannot be led into contradiction. The
person of integrity has identified the points at which he
will stand, not withstanding the consequences. It is
what some mean when they refer to a person as 'really
tough.' We may not agree with him but we respect the
fundamental congruence of his life. He is predictable
not because he is inflexible but because there are certain
areas not open for negotiation."

The greatest loss I've ever suffered is the loss of my
integrity. The deepest personal satisfaction ever to be
mine is when, like a tree planted by the waters, I would
not be moved. This is a large part of what it means to
know who you are. In Atlanta, there is a feisty black
welfare rights lady who was offered $5,000 to endorse
a certain political candidate. She replied, "I don't have
nuthin' but my name and it ain't for sale." God help me
to be that honorable.

The hardest place to be honorable is in your own
backyard. I can be straightforward and brutally blunt at
a university seminar or city-wide political forum. I can
tell it like it is for the television cameras and the radio
microphones. But back home with the folks, it's not so
easy. After all, they pay your salary and you have to live
with them every day.

I bragged to my colleagues about how much freedom

my congregation gave me, but now I must acknowledge that I stayed within boundaries dictated by fear of reprimand.

I criticized major commercial companies for their discriminatory hiring practices, but there was one company I never mentioned. One of our best members had worked there nearly thirty years.

I gave hell to government agencies that victimized poor people with the ridiculous red tape of inept bureaucrats. There was one agency that I hesitated to assail because among their employees was one of our most active church women. The Sunday I did lower the boom, I was relieved to see she was absent.

I needed to call to task the black middle-class snobs who looked down their noses at everyone in their race who hadn't made it yet. But how would that sound coming from a white man?

I walked the middle of the road, forgetting that you get run over by traffic on both sides. I was mostly run over by myself. I lost my self-respect. I sent up trial balloons to see how prophetic I could be, yet knowing all the time that a true prophet does not run around with the latest poll tucked under his arm. I knew I was playing church by consensus in order to gain sanction.

I promised myself better and began to be forthright and plain. I threw my pulpit sophistication to the wind and got rough with some prominent public figures — a state's governor, a country's vice-president, and a worshipped downtown black minister. I accused the governor of blatant racism, the vice-president of splitting the country asunder, and the minister of selling out to insure his prominence in white circles.

Most of our congregation said "Amen." But a few thought the pulpit was no place for such attacks. One lady cornered me.

"What's the big idea?"

"What do you mean?"

"You shouldn't talk about the governor like that."

"Do you agree with his stand?"

"Of course not."

"Then why do you object to my tellin' it like it is?"

"That's all right, but not from the pulpit."

A mild eruption took place when I became more and more vocal about my feeling that we should have gotten out of Viet Nam *yesterday*. There was no compromise in my words and people knew where I stood. One morning, a visitor stalked out of the sanctuary in the middle of my sermon, never to return. A black school teacher told me to keep politics out of the church. A white college professor accused me of oversimplifying issues and thinking from my gut.

Another subject that got me in trouble was birth control. In our community, people have babies like they are going out of style. Children are brought into the world with no hope of their being cared for. Many of those who bring them into the world are themselves children and don't know which end is up. I talked to a 15-year-old about the possibility of a breech birth. "What's a breech?" she replied. I should have expected that, for her mother had an unplanned child at age 40. "Reverend," the mother told me, "I didn't know how to use that stuff the doctor gave me."

Something had to be said about planned parenthood and birth control. I spoke of the pill and of vasectomy. I assisted some young ladies in obtaining legal abortions. I preached a Christmas sermon called, "No Room in the World." I wrote editorials pleading for a more sensible approach.

I know now that the most controversial thing a white man in a black community can do is to come out in favor of birth control.

My neighbor and colleague stopped me as I crossed the street on my way home.

"I read your column this week."

"I'm glad you did."

"Well, I'm not glad I did."

"What's the trouble?"

"I thought you were different, but you're just like every other white man."

"What do you mean?"

"All this crap about birth control. That's just white man's genocide."

"I don't mean it that way."

"Yes, you do. You're just trying to wipe out the whole black race."

He stepped on the gas and sped out of sight. We never talked again.

I had promised myself honesty and was working hard to carry that promise out. I felt free and yet I feared my world was falling apart. I didn't like every Tom, Dick, and Harry taking a pot shot at me. I wondered how many ecclesiastical doors I had closed and if others would ever open up.

Through all of this and much more, my people stayed with me. Surprise! Nobody cancelled his pledge! Nobody withdrew his membership! Nobody boycotted the worship service!

Until — I invited a group called "The African Singers" to be our guests for a special concert. They were black militant youth with hate in their eyes and hostility in their every move. They refused to stay in the homes of our white members. They quickly categorized our whites as "phony liberals" and our blacks as "Uncle Toms." At the concert that night, they sang of killing Mr. Charlie and of canonizing Angela Davis. The last song of the concert was dedicated by the director "from our family on the stage to our family in the audience." One of the singers added, "To the *black* family, that is."

After the concert I took the stage to express my appreciation to our visitors. I told them I had heard their hurt and I hoped everyone else had heard it. I reminded the audience that no man is free until all men are free. I recommitted myself to liberty for the oppressed and invited everyone else to do the same. I meant every word I said. Yet, out of the corner of my eye, I could see some people filing out of the sanctuary in obvious protest. That scared me to death. At that moment I was close to being a free man — and yet so far away.

The next few weeks were accented by tumult and turmoil. The reactions to the singers were as diversified as our congregation. Some whites thought it was great we could have an open forum in a traditionally established, properly connected, obviously institutional

100

church. They had come to East Lake Church to find this freedom and here it was.

Other white people felt put down. They were hurt and offended. For three years, they had worked hard against formidable odds; in a moment it seemed all in vain. (Most of these later rejoiced we were solid enough in fellowship to have the foundations shake a little).

The blacks in the congregation also reacted in different ways. The more militant identified with great emotional kinship to what was said and sung. The young people were particularly in agreement. They were ready to kill Mr. Charlie. Their response was a defiantly clenched-tight fist and an emphatic "Right on, brother!"

Other black people were as offended as were the whites. They feared another overcategorization of all black people. They could hear it coming — "You know how 'they' are." Many blacks were embarrassed for our whites, whose commitment they greatly respected. On the other hand, some blacks were greatly disturbed that some white people had allowed a few racial insults to turn them back a hundred years. They wondered if there were any realness to begin with.

I tried to hear out everyone's feeling and did my best to interpret what I heard. I spoke of every man's right to say what is on his mind. If we do our own thing, that means the other man must be free to do his own thing, even if it conflicts with ours.

I spoke vehemently of the infamy of more than 300 years of inequity and injustice. I reminded everyone of the necessity and validity of black pride, black dignity, and black power. I called all of East Lake Church to a new commitment to invest her energy and resources in the struggle for dignity and humanness.

I also reminded everyone that you don't have to be anti-white to be pro-black. To lump everyone according to color is to name an adversary when you might have an ally. It's not good business. It's certainly a long way from Jesus' gospel of unreserved love for all people.

One white family began an open campaign to discredit me for my complicity in the "fiasco." Right off they said it had ruined our church. Once they had listened to the repercussions, they kept the telephone hot urging more protest and dissension. They demanded I fire our director of music for his involvement in getting the singers to come.

Then, they did what, in my naivete, I thought would never happen at East Lake Church. They threatened to leave and take their money with them.

Now, how free did I want to be? This family was supporting a very large percentage of our small budget all by themselves. How could we make it without them? Perhaps I should have kept my big mouth shut.

I stood my ground, however, and called their bluff. I told them we would not lower our voice to raise our budget. I told them we would miss them but somehow we would get along — we had gotten along before they came.

They weren't bluffing. Pushed by other differences as well, they withdrew their membership and their money. They made a big stink and kept the congregation stirred up for months. Everywhere I went, people could talk of nothing else.

I sat brooding in my study. Yes, I wanted to be a free man and have a free congregation. But at what price? I was so close — and yet so far away. Maybe I'll just go back to business as usual. At that moment, it all seemed very impossible.

CHAPTER 10

When impossibility knocks

There are moments when it all seems impossible. From those first nasty phone calls to the most recent hopeless hassle with city hall, these last five years have been filled with frustration and futility.

I had been warned that there was the stench of death around East Lake Church — and little wonder, what with only 50 members who had agreed to stay, a hundred-thousand-dollar building indebtedness, and a community that was suspicious and hostile. The smell of hopelessness was there, all right.

I picked a member's name from the roll and went to visit. The home was nearby and so I walked. I went with a zip, and returned in a drag. This family had not pledged to stay and serve, but I had hoped to reclaim them. Oh, the naivete of a youthful dreamer!

"Hello, I'm Phil Barnhart from East Lake Church."

"Oh, yeah — you're the one the bishop sent up there to integrate everything."

"I have come to be a minister of the gospel of Jesus Christ."

"We know why you're here. You're here so the niggers can take over our church."

"I'm here to help the church minister to its community."

"Well, it can do it without me. I'm not interested and I'd just as soon you didn't come to my house any more."

I didn't. Impossibility knocks.

I visited several other white families who were members. The reception was much the same.

A white man who had stayed pulled me aside.

"I want to talk with you."

"Sure, what's on your mind?"

"I'm concerned that we don't have many white people here."

"What do you suggest we do about it?"

"Well, I think you're spending too much time with the blacks. You ought to get out and visit the white members and ask them to come back."

I bit my tongue. If he only knew how hard I had tried! Impossibility knocks.

One difficulty that sneaked up on my blind side is that of my own prejudice. At first, I didn't notice it. I was excited, enthusiastic, and caught up in the glamour of my new ministry. Later, when things should have been happening and weren't, I took the easy way out. I blamed the people because they were black. A myriad of myths plummeted from my storehouse of prejudice and I fell victim to the very sin of intolerance which I spent so much time speaking against and acting against.

A dramatic example of this creeping crud of bigotry concerns some young people who had greeted me with

cold stares and blank grunts. I finally got a group of
them together around a pool table, a record player, and
their own four rooms in the church building.

We had met once a week for two years, and one night
after we finished our Bible study, we were cleaning up.
Two teenage girls who had had their differences in the
past were sitting next to each other. One accidentally
bumped the other and a flurry of insults followed. Before I knew what was happening, they were rolling on
the table, pulling hair, scratching, throwing lefts and
rights, and cursing up a storm.

It took all my strength and that of two of our young
men to pull them apart. I tried to talk to them and
finally sent one of them home in order to keep
the peace.

I regained my composure and tried to find out from
the rest of the youth what had happened. I learned
little. We had our closing circle and I packed the group
onto the church bus and took them home.

On my way back, resentment and then anger boiled
up in me. I thought of all the hours and hours I had
spent trying to break through the icy stares and hanging
heads. I recalled trying time and time again to smother
the volatile violence that seemed to be a way of life for
the kids. I remembered thinking that there had been a
squeeze of daylight — a tiny breakthrough. But now my
castles, small as they were, had fallen at my feet. At
first, I was hurt, then mad as hell. When I arrived home
I jumped from the bus, ran across my carport, opened
the kitchen door, and slammed it shut. In the privacy of
my house, I shouted at the top of my lungs: "Those

damn niggers! Those damn niggers!"

I stood in shocked silence. I had never said anything like that before in my life. Impossibility knocks.

Impossibility knocks every time the political and social systems afflict our community's poor people with the cruelty of leftovers and half-hearted promises. Impossibility knocks every time a police officer brutalizes and then asks questions; every time a public housing authority puts 5,000 people into 800 units of concrete jungle, creating a mass and mess of misery; every time you remember that the young man who is sitting on death row would not be there if he were white.

Impossibility knocks when you vow to be your own man and yet know you still ride the ecclesiastical escalator. Impossibility knocks when you brag you are free and yet know there's still a price at which you can be bought. It knocks when you promise your family first priority and instead you ask "How high?" when some disgruntled church member says "Jump!" Impossibility knocks.

When impossibility knocks, who will answer?

Power will answer. Send power to answer.

Send the power of perseverance.

One summer, I took my family to a little cabin in the woods. The first night brought me an impossible assignment: "Daddy, build us a fire so we can roast marshmallows."

I'm not the best fire-builder in the world, but I worked and worked with paper, branches, and logs until a fire was ablaze and the marshmallow-tipped coat hangers were bouncing atop the flames. As I lowered my sweaty body to the floor, a sincere little voice declared, "Daddy, you're our hero."

"Hero" sounded like an awfully large word to assign to such a small feat. Then I remembered a definition of "hero" that I had read. "A hero is no braver than an ordinary man. He's just brave five minutes longer."

In our day, we need heroes — those who are brave five minutes longer. We need those who have the power of perseverance and who know the victory that comes from hangin' on. We need heroes who live in hope for a better day. We need those who have faith in the future, for if there is no faith in the future, there is no power in the present.

There is power in perseverance. There is power in having faith in a God who has gotten you through yesterday to today and will get you through today to tomorrow. There is power in pluggin' away knowing that with God, all things are possible, even the "impossible dream." There is power in the theme of *The Unsinkable Molly Brown*, "I ain't down yet."

In the last five years, I've quit a hundred times and I'm still here. I've been fed up, put out, and teed off. I've walked away from it, only to come back. I've thrown up my hands, then used them to grab the next problem.

Four years ago, our light and gas bills were more than we could pay and we were about to close our weeknight study hall. I was walking home one evening and a little eight-year-old boy ran alongside me and thrust a crumpled envelope into my hand. "Mama says she doesn't want you to close the church," he said. I opened the envelope and out came eight quarters. I knew the family. Those quarters had come hard! We didn't close the study hall. We held on a little while longer out of sheer guts and soon there were enough nickels, quarters, dollars to pay the bill. There is power in perseverance.

After a few months in the East Lake community, I saw that we had to get involved with the reading problems of our children. We had sixth-graders who couldn't read a word. They had sat in overcrowded classrooms and had been socially promoted for six years. I hired a seminary student and enlisted a volunteer. The seminary student missed more sessions than he hit and the volunteer was too much a white, soapbox liberal to face the reality of illiterate children. She wore her involvement as a badge of honor and thought only of the wonderful missionary work she was doing. The program aborted before her eyes. The embryo slipped into my hands and soon miscarried again in a quiet burst of good intentions.

I tried again the next year and was joined by a college professor from First Church. He was the real thing, and there was no miscarriage that year. No birth, but no miscarriage.

The following summer my professor friend, who had since become a member of East Lake Church, joined forces with another academician to launch us on what was to become one of the most meaningful ministries in Atlanta. Our new volunteer was a Ph.D. (married to an M.D.) who quickly became an angel of service as she directed an eight-week summer school over an uncharted course. The results were encouraging.

The next summer we did a little better, and the third

summer we had a jam-up good program resulting in a letter of commendation from the President of the United States. Between summers, we had a variety of reading programs, study halls, and tutorial sessions. Some were fantastic flops, others not quite that bad. The reading program matured into a regular and meaningful part of our ministry and is directed and staffed completely by volunteers.

There were four times when I announced to Margaret Anne I was giving up my dream of a supplementary education emphasis as a hopeless and hapless exercise in futility. But something always happened to recharge me. A few weeks ago, a twelve-year-old boy looked up smilingly at me as I passed him in the hall of a school I was visiting.

I turned to his principal. "How's he doing?"

"Much better."

"He couldn't even read two years ago."

"Your tutors made all the difference in the world."

"And I came so close to just scrapping the whole program."

"Henry's so lucky you didn't."

There is power in perseverance.

There is power in keepin' on keepin' on, not wanting a guaranteed success but only wanting to fulfill one's mission. I begin many things that people pronounce unworkable. Often they don't work. But I must do them anyway. God does not call us to successfulness, but to faithfulness. J. Edward Carothers, in writing of the church's responsibility to convert the cruelty systems of our day, says, "The task of religion is to prepare people for the risks required by sacrificial love, for in the final analysis, there will be no Christian action to convert individuals or cruelty systems unless there are people capable of acting in love in spite of apparently hopeless odds."

There's power in staring impossibility square in the face and saying "I'm still here — I still believe — I still trust — I still hope. You ain't gonna' get me down." I believe in a God who finally got those children through the wilderness even though it took 40 years. They made it, for there came a day when the Lord said, "I set the land before you, go in and possess it." And they did. Yes, there is power in perseverance.

When impossibility knocks, who will answer?

Power will answer. Send power to answer.

Send the power of politics. Perseverance is not enough, for only to stand in gutsy determination is often to stand alone wailing in the forest with no one listening to you. I know! I've been there, brother!

Perseverance must be organized and blended with strategy, tactics, and the strength of others who are also hanging on. We must send to the door on which impossibility knocks the power of politics.

I once thought politics was a dirty word. It's not a dirty *word*, it's a dirty *game*. It's a dirty game because Christians have absented themselves from its arena and have left it to greedy little men who are so busy paying off debts they can't move government to a level where it can participate in the work of God.

A friend of mine confided in me before he announced for a major office, "I'm going to run."

"I think that's great."

"I can make a difference."

"You're a good man."

"My hands are clean."

"How long can they stay that way?"

"When they can't, I'll get out."

"I believe you would get out, but I don't think you'll have to."

He has made a difference. May his tribe increase. We need Christian politicians who will use the power of their office to change the cruelty systems that deny black firemen and black policemen their rights; that spend more money for more plush offices for more inept bureaucrats; that keep public housing ghettoized and the occupants of public housing victimized. We need Christian politicians who will work to change a health system that has never functioned for low-income groups, a money system that makes the poor poorer by charging exorbitant interest rates to people who have to buy or borrow where credit is easy, and every other system that works only for the good of the majority.

We need Christian politicians who will work for moral achievement, seeing their work as a call from a God who is moving in the history of current events — who is moving in the realm of politics. Each of us is obligated to seek out those who are best suited for public office according to the criteria of moral concern and Christian vocation. A clergyman often is in a good position to remind a parishioner of his responsibility and challenge him to become involved. If any minister personally feels a summons from God to throw his own hat in the ring, then let him crank up his campaign and get at it! Politics has become *vocatio* for him, and no call from God should be taken lightly.

Not only do we need Christian politicians, but also political Christians. We need people who will break out of their naivete and be realistic about how conversion is brought about in our day. In the words of Carothers, "The discovery that there are cruelty systems has been accompanied by the discovery that there is only one way to deal with the cruelty inflicted by a system. You have to organize people to change the system or bring in a new one."

For too long, the Christian Church has spoken only of salvation of individuals, forgetting there is such a thing as salvation of systems. For too long, the Christian Church has spoken of saving souls, forgetting that no one's soul will be saved unless there is a conversion of those institutions and structures which forever condemn a man's soul to hell.

Christians must be political, for it is only through the power of politics that we can become the instruments for the salvation which God offers the oppressed and the captives.

The Atlanta Police Department will not improve until Christians organize to put morally sensitive men on the Board of Aldermen and in the Police Department and then lobby constantly to remind them of their duty. A handful of us worked for years to get increased police protection for our area, and it was only when we organized the tenants of a public housing project populated by 5,000 people that we got the results we wanted.

Our ridiculous educational system won't change until we, through our political influence, demand that it be changed. Atlanta was moving this mass of 5,000 people into 800 units of public housing with no school building in sight in which to house the 1,200 elementary children they would bring with them. Our community got itself together and demanded a public meeting with both the school superintendent and the director of public housing present. The angry crowd spoke with such power and intensity that the whole approach was regrouped, and a crash school construction program was begun immediately.

The budget priorities of this country will continue to wave their loyalties toward a military-industrial complex, which clings to an insane war in Viet Nam, until we turn out the senators and congressmen who support such a fiasco and turn in those who will get us out and will divert those billions into programs that will restore the dignity of humanness to those who are losing it while we play with our world power image. We'd still be at full force in Viet Nam if it weren't for the marches, demonstrations, and protests organized and led by concerned Christians. We won't get completely out until we make ourselves felt at the polls, where it really counts.

We can persevere and persist, but until we politick, we are as ineffective as we would be if we repaired a hole in a submarine with screen wire. It's time we Christians stopped *letting* things happen and started *making* things happen. That's done through the power of politics.

But, if, when impossibility knocks, we send only the power of perseverance, we have not sent enough. It will be said we have guts — but intestinal fortitude is not enough to silence impossibility's knock. If we send only the power of politics, we have not sent enough, either. It will be said we are politically astute — but shrewdness is not enough to silence impossibility's knock. If we persevere through politics, we will be both shrewd and steadfast, but more is needed to silence impossibility's knock.

When impossibility knocks, who will answer?

Power will answer. Send power to answer.

Send the power of the Presence. As James Moffatt has said, "We must keep in touch with the fire for the fire always burns." The fire of God's Holy Spirit is the reason "I ain't down yet." Indeed, I have thrown up my hands only to bend my knees in very personal prayer, and then I have risen to take on all comers.

Recently, the residents of the public housing project in our community became put out by the put-offs constantly dealt them by the Atlanta Housing Authority and decided to take matters in their own hands. They arrived early one morning at the management office and took over the entire building, forbidding every employee to enter. They wore their signs of protest and solidified themselves around the door every time someone approached.

Having been in on all the efforts of these people to get decent living conditions, I was in their midst, sporting my sign and adding my body to the human barricade.

Policemen arrived. The sergeant singled me out and took me aside.

"You all have a right to picket."

"I know we do."

"But you don't have a right to take over the building."

"We've done that in order to get the director of housing to come and meet with the people."

"It's still against the law."

"There are unjust laws."

"What you're doin' is wrong."

"What's being done to these people is more wrong."

"I may have to take you to jail."

"I may have to go to jail."

Believe you me, I could not have taken that stand, as right as I knew it to be, had I not felt completely controlled and supported by the power of the Presence. I didn't want to go to jail, but I knew that if I did go, I wouldn't go alone.

There have been many occasions when it all seemed so impossible. The people who left the church — the crank phone calls — the plague of my own prejudice. The severe and continued financial crisis — the dearth of leadership — the hostility of those whom you seek as colleagues and cohorts. The struggle for personal integrity — the fear of being a kept man — the ache for the privacy of my own family. There is much more, but surely by now you have heard my hurt, my anger, my loneliness, my confusion.

I know I'm hurt, angry, lonely, and confused. I have no delusions of peace. I also have no doubts about the work of the Holy Spirit in my life. I follow my Master, a political man who persevered to change the systems that blocked the deliverance of the captives. After five years in an activist stance which has worn me to the ground, I know what Jesus meant when, before he announced the tenets of the platform on which he would run his campaign, he said, "The Spirit of the Lord is upon me."

I know the Lord has laid his hands on me. *Thank you, God, for the power of the Presence. Thank you, God, for miracle after miracle. Thank you, God, for a path before me and the strength to walk in it.*

Once, two ministers were planning a revival and they wanted Dwight L. Moody to be the preacher. The date they had picked conflicted with Moody's schedule. After figuring every way they could to work it out, one of the ministers asked the other, "Why does it have to be Moody? Does Dwight L. Moody have a monopoly on the Holy Spirit?"

"No," replied the other, "but the Holy Spirit has a monopoly on Dwight L. Moody."

God, give us men on whom the Holy Spirit has a monopoly. Then, when impossibility knocks, we can go to the door with the power of perseverance, the power of politics, and the power of the Presence. We can go singing, "Lord, we are able — Our Spirits are thine."

Listen! Impossibility has stopped knocking. Power has gone to answer.

ACKNOWLEDGMENTS

Page 13   From STILL HERE, copyright 1948 by Alfred A. Knopf, Inc. Reprinted from SELECTED POEMS, by Langston Hughes, by permission of Alfred A. Knopf, Inc.

Page 23   From MAN'S SEARCH FOR MEANING by Viktor E. Frankl. Beacon Books, Boston, Mass. 1963.

Page 33   From FAITH IN CONFLICT by Carlyle Marney. Abingdon Press, New York and Nashville, 1957.

Page 41   From VENTURES IN WORSHIP edited by David J. Randolph. Copyright © 1969 by Abingdon Press.

Page 48   From GOOD OLD PLASTIC JESUS by Earnest Larsen, C.SS.R. A LIGUORIAN BOOK, copyright 1968 Liguori, Mo. 63057. Reprinted with permission.

Page 86   From GOD AT LARGE by Chad Walsh. The Seabury Press, New York 1971.

Page 92   From THE COMING FAITH by Carlyle Marney. Abingdon Press, New York and Nashville, 1970.